DO YOU 
YET?
HASE TREK

Do You Feel Numb Yet?

Copyright © 2020 HASE Trek

All rights reserved.

Do You Feel Numb Yet? by HASE Trek. No part of this book may be reproduced in any written, electronic, recording, or photocopying form without written permission of the author, HASE Trek.

Books may be purchased in quantity and/or special sales by contacting the publisher, HASE Trek, by email at Hasetrek@gmail.com.

Editing: Tanisha Stewart
tanishastewart.author@gmail.com

First Edition

Published in the United States of America
by HASE Trek

Table of Contents

Introduction 1

No Not Yet 5

A Little Numb 31

Quite Numb 49

Laws of Numbness 67

Who Else Is Numb? 84

The Wear Off 102

Acknowledgements 107

References 110

Introduction

Drugs have conquered many inner cities and suburbs in today's society. Drug use within various neighborhoods has many dynamics. In the United States, because there is such a variety of drugs, many of its citizens have succumbed to the temporary sense of pleasure they provide. This has led to widespread cases of addiction, which has in turn caused the country to become immersed in an all-out struggle to find order in the prolonged battle with drug containment along with putting a system in place to regulate, delegate rules and accumulate funds associated with it.

With this book, my purpose is to explore, express, inform and enlighten the reader of the importance of being aware of the virulence that drug abuse cultivates.

The approach of this read will not be to blame a specific entity or group. Instead, my goal is to intentionally take an abstract stance to allow for individuals who may have been influenced or affected by drug abuse to utilize the information provided in the most positive befitting way. I am including insightful data, conjoined with authentic comparisons from actual people's realities to allow for an increase in awareness of this phenomenon.

The United States is a nation that prides itself on the maintenance of select nationalities; however, it also has an apprehension toward its responsibility of ensuring the same liberties for other nationalities. In other words, when it comes to the drug epidemic, black drug users are seen as criminals, while whites are viewed through a lens of privilege, and therefore are afforded more resources and opportunities to help break their addictions. Because of this, I will engage in a deliberate exploration of criminal disparities with regard to race, in addition to a discussion of the histories of various drugs which have been a part of the drug epidemic.

Containment of widespread drug usage has been difficult for the U.S. over the past few decades, from witnessing it to actually lying within its fury. The mass drug issue extends beyond race – it is a humanity issue – however, it is viewed with indifference in many circles. Every sub-population that has suffered from widespread abuse of drugs has endured much - either as a result of numerous fatalities caused by overdosing; medically, as in health problems due to prolonged abuse; or legally, as a result of many abusers having to be encompassed in the court system due to the laws against it.

DO YOU FEEL NUMB YET?

All three in some cases.

Despite the fact that drug abuse is prevalent in many communities across the United States, according to popular opinion, there is one population of people that are generally believed to be most affected: Blacks.

To this idea, much can be synthesized to get down to the core of a crucial issue. Not a mystery right? Melanated people have been labeled by society as the front-runners for drug use and abuse as well as the distribution of illegal drugs and have been disproportionately chastised by the laws of this nation after being conditioned to participate in an unworthy cause as a result of these labels. Contrarily, beyond the surface information we receive through media, many studies show contrary results and allow for a clearer analytical observation of the phenomenon of widespread drug abuse, rather than relying upon racial stereotypes.

Headlines such as these convey a history of the manipulation of the public's views toward Blacks by the media:

On NBC News, "Painkiller Use Breeds New Face of Heroin Addiction" (Schwartz, 2012), and also "The New Face of Heroin Addiction" (ABC News, 2010). Some are extremely insensitive like in the article, "Negro Cocaine 'Fiends' Are a New Southern Menace: Murder and Insanity Increasing Among Lower Class Blacks Because They Have Taken to 'Sniffing' Since Deprived of Whisky by Prohibition" which was published in the New York Times in February 1914 by Edward Huntington Williams, (Williams, 1914).

We've seen this type of manipulation in the media throughout history via the use of code words. Code words are words we tend to bypass simply due to a lack of understanding of their meanings which unconsciously reinforce the biases utilized to differentiate societal drug abuse within communities. The terms 'urban' and 'suburban' are often intently used to differentiate between black and brown communities as compared to white communities.

Do You Feel Numb Yet? intends to effectively focus on certain aspects of drugs, drug addiction, and the social discrepancies tied to drug addiction. It deliberately focuses on social circumstances, types of substances frequently abused, the historical aspects of drug abuse, and real-life accounts of individuals who have a history with drugs. This book is dynamic due to the information synthesized within it. Though the information presented is precise and accurate, the reader is encouraged to consciously reflect on the various topics discussed for the sake of understanding and application of the provided material.

No Not Yet

Oftentimes I ponder how in the hell drugs were introduced to my community close to 70 years ago and how we still have barely managed to find a way to overcome the beast of drug addiction.

I grapple with not just how, but why this epidemic has been so successful in terms of the destruction, despair and anguish it has caused. As I recall trekking through my native streets of Newark, NJ, I encountered so many fathers and mothers who were damaged badly as a result of drug abuse. Having once been lives of promise, full of hope and potential, what now remains is an aberrant shell of a community, resulting from a maladaptive phenomenon that has had intergenerational impacts.

Full family trees, decaying limbs and branches, barely surviving from the poison of the beast. Parents, grandparents, aunts and uncles… the list continues and is so widespread. Drugs have simply ravaged the dynamics of the once firm components of the family tree. The beast of addiction is indiscriminate. Lack of mental prowess has rendered so many of its victims defenseless to the inevitability of drug addiction, a slippery slope that spring-boarded into a variety of resulting issues in families.

Growing up, I saw very clearly that drugs were a problem. I didn't want to be associated with them or the effects that they caused. However, it is impossible to avoid or block out what stands before you every day. Drug abuse or addiction is a major force. Although the drugs may have come from other areas outside of Newark, or even outside of the United States, the fact that they devastated my community was evident in my day to day interactions with many drug abuse victims.

From heroin, to crack cocaine, to pill popping and cough syrup soda mixing, people are and have been subjecting themselves to theses vices for decades, despite the increasing availability of resources and information that are designed to educate them about the effects of drug use and abuse.

In addition to resources and education, drug users have undoubtedly seen the effects of abuse with their own eyes through friends and members of their families that have succumbed to its pressures. Awareness of drug abuse in my upbringing was as common as a cold in Newark, NJ. This continued throughout my maturation to adulthood. Familiarity

DO YOU FEEL NUMB YET?

with drug use and abuse in the inner city allowed for myself and my neighborhood peers to accept it, adjust it and conform to the concept of drug addiction.

Many of my peers could not see beyond what they saw in their day to day lives. When you live in a certain environment and this type of lifestyle is prevalent, it only makes sense that people will have a tendency to repeat the patterns of behavior that have been set before them.

The problem is two-fold: Not only has the drug epidemic become a major issue for the communities that have been affected by it, it also seems that there is minimal assistance being provided to the affected communities from those who have the ability and resources to help resolve the issue. I believe that it is the moral, legal, and social responsibility for those that have the ability to provide these needed resources to make a greater effort to ensure that they are getting to the people who need them.

Lack of adequate help has caused communities to live in increasingly devastated conditions. When one steps foot in any "urban" community, what you see is not what you see when you enter a suburban community. The people, landscape and overall quality of living are contradictory between the two types of communities.

In today's society, social living conditions still are relevant, as can be seen in the case of the Flint water crisis. Flint - a proletariat city once known for its industrial prowess, is now a hub for poverty. The tainted water supply in its black communities depicts how one's ethnicity or color can impact the support or resources that are provided to adequately assist families. Flint getting minimal help despite the national coverage on its water crisis spotlights the grand issue of 'black problems' versus 'white problems'.

Returning to the discussion of drug addiction and/or abuse, similar to the Flint situation, blacks are not treated with the same level of interest in their social issues as white people.

In 1986, the Anti-Drug Abuse Act, establishing how the weight or amount of illegal drug possession required for specific criminal charges to be administered sounded like a great way to control illegal drug use and distribution. Unfortunately, the results of this act were quite different from its proposed intentions. The outcome of such a law was crafty terms and stipulations within that law aimed to negatively impact specific communities of color:

"So in 1986, Congress passed the Anti-Drug Abuse Act establishing, for the first time, mandatory minimum sentences for those convicted of having specific amounts of cocaine. The sentences, however, were much tougher for crack cocaine than powder cocaine cases — which disproportionately affected African-Americans" (Glanton, 2017).

DO YOU FEEL NUMB YET?

    This disease though, is different… It doesn't select a person or a people - it does not discriminate in any shape, form, or fashion. We often hear the saying that 'bullets don't have names on them' – well, neither do drugs. Like stray bullets from a gun, drugs affect not only those who intentionally use them, but they have the potential to negatively impact those surrounding the users or abusers as well.

    Once an individual succumbs to drug abuse, his or her image becomes distorted. The drugs take control over his or her life, and the abuser becomes a puppet pulled in various directions by the influence of the disease.

    During my younger years, I wasn't aware that there were so many different varieties of drugs. However, as I grew older, I began to learn that not only were there different types of drugs, each drug had a different type and level of effect on its user – a different 'high', so to speak. It was inevitable that I was exposed to this information because there were members of my family who were drug users and abusers. Even in my attempts to distance myself from the devastating reach of the disease, it was inescapable due to the people I was surrounded by.

    As a boy transforming into a man, my fascination with drug culture increased. I became influenced by my environment. The introduction to drugs from a young age, the glorification of it through media outlets, and various life situations that seemed to challenge my adamant pursuits all worked together to influence my decision-making.

Movies, music and video games consistently embedded drugs in my brain, whether it was in the songs I sang, movies I watched or video games like Grand Theft Auto, containing graphic material like guns, sex and drugs. As I grew into an adult, I encountered situations such as job loss, bill accumulation, power-seeking and pure loss of self. These are all triggers that can lead one to that ever readily available realm of drugs. Drugs were a readily available coping mechanism.

From my own cognizance of drugs, a majority of the inhabitants in this country's first experience started rather early. In many cases, people are introduced to at least one illicit substance by the time they become a teen. The teen years are the realm of life where many assume that life is supposed to work to their liking and that it is to be lived freely.

Teens often seek to be free-spirited. Adolescence is a stage of life where teens make a number of independent decisions. Some decisions that they make should be carefully weighed to determine the possible effects they may cause; however, unfortunately this does not happen on a large scale. Instead, many teens are more focused on being cool, relevant, or daring rather than being safe or educated. This usually results in them attempting to consume, ingest or

DO YOU FEEL NUMB YET?

engulf themselves in a substance with damaging effects as wells as physically disproportionate repercussions.

Teens are apt to experiment with drugs as a result of having lesser developed brains and their susceptibility to become easily influenced.

This is an intriguing concept to mention. In addition to the fact that teens are more susceptible to the influence of drug use, think of the price and accessibility of drugs for teens. During my adolescent years, much of my ignorance about drugs influenced my faulty behavior. Teens are still kids, though many believe they are adults mentally. They often don't maintain the capacity to make strong cognitive decisions. Researchers have reported that 25 years of age is when the brain reaches its full potential:

"18 year olds are about halfway through that process. Their prefrontal cortex is not yet fully developed. That's the part of the brain that helps you to inhibit impulses and to plan and organize your behavior to reach a goal... Which it reaches around age 25 and that makes adolescents and young adults more interested in entering uncertain situations to seek out and try to find whether

there might be a possibility of gaining something from those situations

(Aamodt, 2011)."

In congruity, an article by **Winters and Arria (2018)** stated that,

"Furthermore, certain conditions may be ripe for risk taking by teenagers. These include situations in which a teenager is experiencing high emotion, in the presence of intense peer pressure, and faced with a perception that a short-term reward or positive outcome will be obtained. In these situations, the still-maturing "brake" circuitry in the front part of the brain may be particularly overwhelmed by the "accelerator" region compromising the ability to make thoughtful decisions."

This is something to take into consideration when thinking of teens around the world or in one's family the next time they make an impulsive decision.

Many can still remember the commercials which instructed us that if we smoked weed, our brains would become equal to a fried egg in a pan, with no real attachment to what that meant. As a result, the only dependable credible

DO YOU FEEL NUMB YET?

assistance I had in understanding drugs and their effects was the real-life observations within my immediate environment.

As I grew older, I began to challenge these commercials because I, as well as many of my peers, became more aware of drugs due to the prevalence of them in our communities. The effects that I saw firsthand assured me that drugs were indeed bad. However, I reasoned that not all substances labeled "drugs" applied to this though. I was not completely erroneous when coming to such a decision. But when the drugs established as 'bad' drugs were involved, I understood that there was a higher probability of causing more intense imperil. The following is an example of an experience I had which helped me to distinguish which drugs were considered to be "bad":

At the age of 11, I was sitting down in the kitchen, one-half of an Italian cheesesteak resting on the transparent tabletop, the other half resting in the palms of my hands as I savored every bite of this delicious sandwich that my grandma got me from the Chicken Shack… I was filled with pure bliss as I attempted to devour this meal.

Then, out of nowhere…

In a scurry, breezing past me comes one of my aunts. The stove clicks four times, and ignites. She packs her pipe up with 'diesel' as she calls it, puts it on the flame, and inhales and exhales a few times.

HASE TREK

That oh, so delicious cheesesteak loses its taste and I freeze in almost disbelief as to what just happened.

Suddenly, my aunt looks at me, then requests $3 from me.

Still in shock, I barely get a word out. She shrugs me off, then hurries back out of the house. Replaying the events in my mind, I was thinking, Wow. This is getting bad with her. Minutes later, I eased back into my sandwich, but my thoughts were clouded as to the events that transpired.

Another tear in the shield of innocence which, doesn't last long for people in my community.

Imagine what followed. Many of you reading this book may not need to imagine because the reality is you've either witnessed it or live in it on a daily basis.

As a kid, this was a tough reality to cope with. Honestly, I'd convinced myself that this was normal and not to tell anyone else about what happened because of the commotion that would follow if I spoke on it. So, I just held it in and used it as a visual memory to resist "bad" drugs. Though my aunt was a nearby example, there were various others in close proximity to me that reminded me of the negatives of crack cocaine and the risks of drug abuse.

Crack cocaine, heroin and PCP were drugs that are 'no go's'.

Physical displays of "crack heads", "sherm" addicts, and all variety of drug fiends was drug education beyond what a

DO YOU FEEL NUMB YET?

D.A.R.E video would attempt to teach me. Consciously by the age of 12, I'd only begun to see one drug that didn't transform individuals into an aged, deformed and mentally challenged being: Marijuana, weed, chronic, green, or whatever one prefers to name it.

Everywhere you go, there is a different slang term for it. Rather than "frying your brain," weed smokers were pretty chill and equal to cool in my eyes. Hipsters, Woodstock, rappers and movies showed me that the weed smokers were cool. Listening to Stevie Wonder's Hotter Than July album catching a reference in his music to getting high off the happy plant, or Styles P's "I Get High", or Snoop Dogg being crowned an ambassador of weed helped to develop my rationale.

As optimistic as marijuana use looks due to its health advantages and other purposes, there is a concern there. Advocacy for the coolness of the plant doesn't take from the effects it can have on you as well, even though they are not as severe as with other drugs. Marijuana can cause hallucinations, paranoia, memory and processing delays, and impaired body movement as stated by Drugabuse.gov (2019), all of which wear off as the euphoric experience is decreasing due to the time elapsing. There have also been numerous reports as to marijuana stunting brain development if consumed consistently at a young age.

My earliest recollections of consciously seeing weed consumed was age 12. I would occasionally go to my cousins' home where her boyfriend would indulge in marijuana use. Observing his mannerisms was vital to developing my perceptions of the drug because he seldom was lazy or lethargic. He was a father of two kids, had two full time jobs and a girlfriend. The green plant was always a part of his daily tasks. A true champion in my eyes, he was active enough in the home to educate his daughters, cook, clean, and provide all other necessary duties to maintain a home in addition to working two jobs weekly.

Just to clarify, in no way am I promoting drug usage by telling this story, because we should weigh all aspects and options with regard to anything we do in life.

Fast forward to today, where weed is the overly popularized drug if any is said to be. The extensive uses for weed now allow for over half the USA to participate in the development and monetizing of its crops. Not to forget the consumption of the plant. Major business profits have been achieved with this plant by transitioning it from a street drug to crediting it for its health purposes. In other words, widespread efforts in changing the cognitive understanding of the drug has largely led the public to accept it as helpful rather than harmful, despite the fact that the drug itself has not changed.

From aches, pains, terminal ailments, anxiety disorders, or whatever you can think of, marijuana is now utilized in various forms. It is likely to be smoked, or in other cases eaten. Weed, also in alignment with genetic modifications

DO YOU FEEL NUMB YET?

such as CBD allows for cannabidiol, aka CBD, to be extracted from the plant form, which can be turned into creams, oils, candies, juices, and the list continues. Even allowing for people to get stocks in cannabis or cannabis-related avenues like lighting companies, soil companies, distributers and cultivators around the world.

But prior to this explosive rally behind weed was a major campaign as previously stated to combat weed consumption, distribution and to impose mind-boggling criminal penalties against those in proximity or possession of it. **The grass hasn't always been greener.** You get it?

Weed, the "gateway drug", is the choice for most early drug users, yet at such an early age, this is a problem because the deceptiveness of the perceived lack of harmful effects of it can lead teens to feel likewise with more dangerous drugs.

"Adolescents are "biologically wired" to seek new experiences and take risks, as well as to carve out their own identity. Trying drugs may fulfill all of these normal developmental drives, but in an unhealthy way that can have very serious long-term consequences" (National Institute on Drug Abuse, 2014).

HASE TREK

Curiosity and adolescence go hand in hand. That same curiosity may have steered me to the semi-legal substance too. As shown in the above-mentioned research, it is not uncommon for young teens to experiment with risky behaviors such as drug use. Drugs can catapult a life down a path of pain. The chase for that thrill, or urge to act on their curiosity, resulting in an unpleasant experience, satisfied experience or immediate absorption in drug usage.

Take for instance a young brother who was well known in my community of Newark, NJ. Full of potential, vibrant and once a possible candidate to be a professional athlete, he is now faced with dismantled aspirations at the whim of the monkey latched to his back, diminishing that sparkle in his eye only to replace it with a desolate stare. One mishap fueled by peer pressure led to lifestyle changes as a 27 year-old-dope addict. Sad stories like this are all too common and have been since the 60's.

Cognitive maturity of individuals under the age of 25 is at risk with the impulse to participate in substance abuse. Sad to say, the young man may not redeem himself or bounce back from a mistake such as casual weed smoking. One interesting point is that contaminated materials on marijuana may not be visible to the eye so this explains why someone would think they are smoking solely weed. Many times, users are unaware of it being laced or manipulated.

DO YOU FEEL NUMB YET?

Andy LaFrate, Ph.D. (2015) explains, "It's pretty startling just how dirty a lot of this stuff is," he says. "You'll see a marijuana bud that looks beautiful. And then we run it through a biological assay, and we see that it's covered in fungi."

Confirming that NOT all tainted weed is detectable by the naked eye.

Black communities commonly self-medicate to deal with adverse living circumstances. Along with self-medicating can come unfortunate mishaps like addiction, death, overdosing and severe bodily harm. The best bet is to stay away from drugs. There is no need to take chances with your well-being.

Heavily salient in black communities combating drug dominance for decades upon decades is the actuality that drugs have been deep seated in the communities. Side effects of drugs may be overwhelming or life changing in the sense they often cause one's body to be put in unsafe predicaments. Remember that the body is adapting to an experience where one's natural chemistry is being altered simply for pleasure. Things don't always go according to plan when one commits to getting high.

According to the National Institute on Drug Abuse (2019), "Marijuana over activates parts of the brain that contain the highest number of these receptors."

This causes the "high" that people feel." Leading to mood swings, distorted memories, irregular body movements, hallucinations and in some cases, psychosis. Weed has the ability to create an unpleasant experience for users. Even in my first self-published book <u>Circle of Pain</u> on Amazon.com, I disclose an experience at college where I'd just smoked some weed that someone gave me that created such an unpleasant experience that I had my roommate call an ambulance, and then after going to the hospital, it basically was summed up to be a bad trip or high.

It was more importantly a lesson that I needed to slow down and reevaluate my decisions and priorities. Who is to say that the weed was not laced or that it was just weed that I smoked? I trusted my peers to make the best choice for me, but can we always be sure that they will? **Make sure you make the correct choice when it comes to peer pressure or influence.**

Drug usage involving adolescents or young adults is prevalent due to reasons such as emotional mismanagement, acceptance-seeking among peers and lack of comprehension of the serious effects of drugs in general.

DO YOU FEEL NUMB YET?

"46% of all high school students currently use addictive substances, and 12% meet the clinical criteria for addiction" (Center on Addiction, 2011).

In conjunction, almost half of all high school populations in the US use addictive substances, i.e. marijuana, alcohol, cocaine and cigarettes. Studies reveal that 1 in 4 Americans who began using any addictive substance before age 18 become dependent on drugs, compared to 1 in 25 who started using at age 21 or older. Early drug usage simply is more damaging than later drug usage, though both are bad. Dependency on drugs is more common with younger age experimentation than older age experimentation (Center on Addiction, 2011).

Drugs in the teen culture is a major problem and it coincides in today's society with the influx of suicides.

In a survey done in the United States,

"Suicide is the 4th most common cause of death among 10–14 year old's, and the 3rd most common cause of death among 15–24 year old's (Anderson and Smith, 2003).

Our youth are becoming incapable of handling life stressors and are damaging themselves as a result of lacking effective coping skills. Teens are conducting themselves like adults when it comes to social issues: Allowing for substance consumption to regulate emotions. Leading to unforeseen impacts in one's own life. The youth population's contribution to addictive substances is a major issue and even going into a deeper analysis is the influence of race in addictive substances as well as the stigmas tied to specific cultures.

When race is aligned with statistics, they show a contrast in cultures through the consumption of drugs by choice. Similarities can be quite surprising as well.

"Marijuana usage rates were nearly identical among white and African-American adolescents; about 21 percent of high school seniors from both racial/ethnic groups reported usage in 2009" (Stagman, Schwartz, & Powers, 2011).

While there are great similarities between different cultures involving substance use, the most notable differences are the emotional and conscious internalization while or after the substance begins to regulate one's behavior. The free-spirited consumption aiding in reckless, excessive and careless actions without repercussions seems to allow white teens to get the most out of their inebriation without negative labeling attached to them. Meanwhile for other cultures, the display of similar characteristics cause them to be held in a

DO YOU FEEL NUMB YET?

different regard, with mainly negative connotations use to stigmatize them.

I bore witness to this in my early college days, where I would see many of my white friends display a freeness beyond just "getting wasted".

In most scenarios, this resulted in reckless, impulsive and irrational decision-making. Comportment beyond the ability to consciously regulate oneself. Frequent major blackouts and regurgitations at numerous festive events. Followed by a recollection of their wonderful experience upon crossing paths with them again.

One day, I recall sitting in my Media and Cinema Studies class when a conversation about drug use came up and ultimately the broad conversation narrowed in on a few courageous classmates who talked about their experiences growing up in suburban areas battling cocaine and heroin use at 16 and 18 years old.

All were white and felt super accomplished to have been able to reflect on such a dark part of their lives. Reflecting on my teen experience, rarely were young adults in my neighborhood addicted to hard drugs because of the physical and mental damage we witnessed in our black communities as a result of generational drug use.

Much of white teen's freeness to get inebriated beyond belief too is aligned with the media, movies and music they listen to. Artists like Limp Bizkit, Kid Rock, Kiss, and also movies like Animal House, The Hangover, Super Bad and the news showing extreme intoxicated behavior at championship victories like World Series, Super bowl, and NBA finals all entice the actions of white teens to act accordingly. The difference that is often seen between the influence of drug use on black and white teens is that white teens have more ready access to resources to help battle drug addiction than black teens.

White people know or simply assume that they will have the necessary backing or resources to get the help they need when challenges arise. Which in most occasions works out in such a manner.

"White suburban youth were heavier users of tobacco products, alcohol, and inhalants, and experienced more difficulties with blackouts, family conflict, school absence, suicidal ideation, and loss of peer relationships" (Farrow & Schwartz, 1992).

It's interesting that though white people do have privilege, the reality is that all people deal with struggle and pain, even if it is solely internal, and even if their economic status allows for a better quality of living. The commonalities between numerous cultures related to substance abuse shows how immense and widespread of an issue it is. Tobacco, weed and alcohol become the initial drug

DO YOU FEEL NUMB YET?

engagement for most teens, especially black teens. Emotion suppressers like drugs are easily accessible in black communities.

Teens associate maturity with smoking and drinking along with other vices because adults display these behaviors on the norm.

I too was reeled in, thus inhaling and exhaling the earth-grown hippy plant very frequently by my late teen years. As sketchy as any drug had ever been to me, I'd still take the chances, though reluctantly due to my family's struggle with crack cocaine and heroin abuse. Nevertheless, the "curiosity bug" found its way to me.

The ease at which one is put when they consume weed is a feeling that can become a thrill to seek either constantly or periodically. On the contrary, knowing that any risk of consuming weed could be detrimental in a sense of becoming addicted to it or being persuaded to try stronger substances is a source of concern, though thankfully I had major reluctance to ever going to hard core drugs.

Between me and my friends, smoking weed was not harmful. For one, it brought us together, made us comical and became something we all could relate to. In the early 2000's, it was still considered to be a very dangerous drug but for us, it was our secret life, our start of manhood. Yet the potential consequences if we were caught by police or our parents constantly intruded on such a calculated risk. At times too much weed would lead to extreme drowsiness, feeling lethargic, paranoia and dehydration. Beyond the various pleasantries I experienced from it, this is not an advocacy or promotion of weed. **Anything that can become addictive can become a PROBLEM.**

"Cultural and societal norms influence acceptable standards of substance use. Public laws determine the legality of the use of substances. Substance-related disorders in adolescence are caused by multiple factors including genetic vulnerability, environmental stressors, social pressures, individual personality characteristics, and psychiatric problems. However, determining which of these factors are most to blame in adolescent populations has not been determined" (Stagman, Schwartz, & Powers, 2011).

Life can overwhelm an individual to the point that irrationality becomes the rational. As a teen, I think one's awareness of many things becomes evident and many are not able to cope with some of the things they may learn. With a combination of difficulties, the need for an escape can be ever so demanding. Creating a way to instantly escape reality without actually relocating increases the need for drugs. So we're presented with problems, where there are tons of better

DO YOU FEEL NUMB YET?

ways to resolve them, but the easiest way for an individual to find resolve is to drug them away. **Choose Wisely...**

"Homelessness is a significant risk factor for substance use. The majority of homeless youth on the streets use substances such as tobacco (81 percent), alcohol (80 percent), or marijuana (75 percent)" (Greene, Ennett, & Ringwalt, 1997).

Newark, NJ, my native land, is an inner city with homelessness dispersed throughout. Teen homelessness in the city pipelines straight to gang activity, drug usage, and drug selling, while funding prisons throughout the state.

Rational and moral reasoning's presence are bleak. The crucial responsibility of having to utilize idle time when you rarely understand it is detrimental. Lack of understanding as such will strongly entice an individual to succumb to the fishline of influence. This unevenly tips the scales with regard to witnessing the linkage between one's community and drug abuse. Poverty never lost its prevalence in the community of Newark since the 60's; likewise with numerous other black cities.

Sadly, many cities are utilizing reform and reconstructing tactics to re-design financial sectors in these impoverished cities while still leaving the outskirts desolate and dilapidated. Red-lined war zones, crime ridden districts, under resourced

HASE TREK

on every spectrum, distortion of this magnitude complicates extrication from such disparity. The lethargic physical makeup of the outskirts of the financial district should receive the same attention as other areas that are deemed "more important" for the sake of their financial potential.

Flashing back mentally to the scenery I'd grown up in, I imagine a trek through the sector distancing Frelinghuysen Avenue from Newark, NJ from Newark Ave in Elizabeth, NJ.

Dreary, discolored roads filled with hallowed souls. Blended with notorious activities of dope dealing, sex-selling and dilapidated buildings. Newark is a proletariat city with rich history. Much of which is unspoken of. Many of the people who live in Newark do not discuss their knowledge about Newark. Many are uninformed about the city beyond the Newark riots which we know of only because the story was passed down to us like a victory, though much hasn't changed positively since then for black communities.

Homelessness and poverty gleefully run through inner city neighborhoods defeating individuals. Much of the homelessness is tied to the use of addictive substances. I'm quite sure many people within inner cities are facing challenges whether by overwhelming bill accumulation, low paying toxic jobs, unhealthy relationships, trauma untreated and lack of knowledge of self. Conditions that will lure anyone into some form of escape.

DO YOU FEEL NUMB YET?

Unfortunately, the most frequent escape is alcohol, tobacco and illegal drugs. Alcohol, illegal drugs and tobacco are on just about every corner in the hood. Lack of adequate resources and mechanisms to cope with emotions, stress and external factors is the true gateway to drug addiction or any substance abuse.

"Addictive disorders disrupt relationships with family and friends and often cause people to lose their jobs. A 2008 survey by the United States Conference of Mayors asked 25 cities for their top three causes of homelessness. Substance abuse was the single largest cause of homelessness for single adults (reported by 68% of cities). Substance abuse was also mentioned by 12% of cities as one of the top three causes of homelessness for families" (National Coalition for the Homeless, 2009).

With homelessness being considered 'the bottom' for most, add drug abuse to it. Could one imagine the countercurrent actions needed to be taken to regain some form of normalcy to one's life? If stress had been a factor for substance abuse, imagine the stress behind trying to regain control of one's life in efforts to make substance abuse easier to cope with or overcome. Most of the time when people see a homeless person, it is assumed that their homelessness is related to drug or substance abuse.

As reported by Didenko andPankratz (2007),

"Research reveals that approximately two-thirds of homeless people cite alcohol and/or other drugs as a major, and at times primary, reason for becoming homeless."

Dreadfully, speculating that a person who is homeless is in the situation due to substance abuse may indeed be an accurate guess based on the statistic above alluding to the idea that 67% of individuals are. To avoid such a crisis, consider your circumstances and come up with a logical plan to alter your situation for the positive. **Negate drugs as a possible solution.**

A Little Numb

"JUST SAY NO" was the implementation of prevention through verbal response against the pressures of illegal substance use. Utilized by the Reagan administration, the D.A.R.E. program proceeded, which according to History.com (2017), was created by Daryl Gates, an LAPD police Chief, as a response to the rampant drug problem in black and brown neighborhoods. D.A.R.E. was a vivid memory in my mind as many others. The 90's era was a crucial time to be raised and developed in.

 Upon viewing a D.A.R.E. video, complacent, sitting upright with my fingers woven together, widely alert as my eyes attracted to the large pizza-box-shaped screen. The TV, detracting our narrow mindedness with these situational clips of kids succumbing to temptation leading to experimentation of various drugs. From that point on, it was assumed by my teachers and those who created the film that I'd become more competent in understanding what was happening in my community from a made-up scenario.

    False.

    I was baffled that this was even a part of life and the randomness of the school to show us a video of kids being introduced to drugs was overwhelming in a sense.

"Despite the program's popularity, several studies have shown participating in D.A.R.E. has little impact on future drug use" (History.com Editors, 2017).

    Decades later, I can recall everything about the eerie video we watched that was intended to help us, so they thought. After viewing the video, I should have been able to identify the linkage between substances and the stigmas tied to each drug. Instead, I simplified it in my mind that "drugs are bad". So the video really didn't adhere to its plan to educate; it merely introduced us to the problems going on in our communities with no solutions or real break down.

    Lack of knowledge or understanding fuels ignorance. I along with others were not aware of the real issue or reason of the videos. The lack of ability to effectively and thoroughly process the information made the D.A.R.E. initiative ineffective. Totally losing its grip on the mission to educate for the purpose of prevention.

DO YOU FEEL NUMB YET?

"In 2001, the Surgeon General of the United States, Dr. David Satcher, put D.A.R.E. in the category of "ineffective primary prevention programs" (History.com Editors, 2017).

Seeing that 75% of schools used the D.A.R.E. program, as per History.com (2017), and that no real change has risen from it shows its lack of influence in the nation.

On the contrary D.A.R.E. advocates feel differently.

"**Proponents of D.A.R.E. have called some of the studies flawed and say surveys and personal accounts reveal that the program does in fact have a positive effect on future drug use**" (History.com Editors, 2017).

With experts in drug prevention and influence unsure of its accuracy, think about how the communities impacted by drug abuse feel.

How to make sense of D.A.R.E.?

Realizing that maybe this was not the best way to counteract the major drug problem existing in black communities. It was, in a sense, more enticing to an individual to discover more of what these so-called drugs were about.

Many of our family members were deeply involved in the world of which we were not fully aware of.

D.A.R.E. made you want to find out who was using what, and why? Then seek them out for the 'real deal' answers. A theory as to why drug abuse grew was because of individuals comparing community perspectives on certain drugs and not doing further research past word of mouth.

"A study funded by the Department of Justice, which was released in 1994, revealed that partaking in D.A.R.E. led to only short-term reductions in the use of tobacco but had no impact on alcohol or marijuana use" **(History.com Editors, 2017).**

Coexistence with the beast ravaging throughout the community baffles those who have no insight about those who have been conquered by the beast.

Drug abusers are human, and society should be able to see that beyond their demented appearance. No D.A.R.E. video could clarify what needed to be comprehended. When I think of the lost connection between the drug user and those who don't abuse drugs, there is a margin. All perceptions of someone is formed in the mind on the basis of agreements and disagreements.

Most are taught if you are morally flawed, naturally we disagree with you and this type of thinking leads to the

DO YOU FEEL NUMB YET?

concept that drug addicts are bad people who are unworthy of respect.

Drug users wear flaws a lot more openly then the rest of us.

Growth within society educated me contrastingly, enabling me to identify those who struggled with drug addiction with dignity, moving them out of the pariah realm. These people too had big ambitions, major talents and dreams they would have liked to fulfill. We all see glimpses within our neighborhood as in the case of the 27-year-old basketball phenom that I previously mentioned, or the guy who landscapes the lawns on the blocks, or the guy who does carpentry or paints like in the case of my dad, who is a drug abuser.

These people have positive attributes that we aren't quick to acknowledge. Sadly, they were not able to reach their full potential because of their succumbing to drugs. The potential for positive change is there, and it's possible to be achieved with a commitment to altering one's lifestyle. Many tend to avoid that option as we see daily.

When identifying substance abusers we tend to only look at their current state which deals with their maturity. But as disclosed earlier in the book much of their initial partaking in substance abuse often happens quite earlier in their lives. To look at the mature addict is to look at the adolescent addict. Initially, most drug abusers or addicts began at a young age,

"According to reports by the Substance Abuse and Mental Health Services Administration (2014), many children are already engaging in drug activity at age 12 or 13, henceforth understanding that there is a strong probability that they've been using earlier than that."

Quite scary, correct?

That's why constant involvement in your children's life is crucial during their pre-teen/teen ages. As a parent, the more a child matures, the influence and consistency of the parent carries a heavier load. Experience and information is to be relayed consistently while maintaining a parents' standards within their children's lives. This is not to insinuate that parents should be their child's friend solely, but that parents should help to guide their children's moral compass when it comes to the balance of societal issues and outside expectations toward negative influences.

Parents, friends and loved ones should feel free to always ask questions, randomly check in, inform, and always be available to children to ensure they are getting all the prevention and education needed when involving this issue.

"Be consistent. Set clear and concise rules about not using drugs. Your children will come to you when they

hear things like, "everybody drinks", or "marijuana is harmless; it's even legal in some states". Your rules reflect your family's beliefs and principles, not everyone else's" (Adams, 2017).

Parents must understand the importance of healthy relationships with regard to them and their children. Talks are very effective in this manner. Parents should know who their children are socializing and bonding with. Peer influence, as discussed, is a major factor to early drug experimentation and addiction. As a parent, be able to pinpoint who are positive and negative influencing factors in your kids' lives. Which is another way to prevent drug use for your kids. Be unafraid to go through your child's belongings to know who and what your child's interests are.

"Be there. Pay attention to what your children are consuming with regard to television shows, movies, the Internet and video games. There is a lot of inappropriate content that children will become exposed to that is almost impossible to avoid. It is in the way you take the opportunity to discuss these messages that will affect how children perceive and react to them" (Adams, 2017).

As kids mature to pre-teen and teen years, entertainment becomes a major influence on them, so definitely be aware of the social media, music and TV content being consumed. Go watch TV or sit in the room with your children to observe their interests and habits during leisure time. Some parents may feel it is not a right thing to do, but you can gain more knowledge about your children by rummaging through their belongings whether while they are away from you or outright in front of them.

With stress and rebellion contributing as reasons to partake in drug or substance abuse, parents, resolve issues with your children in a mutually understanding way, and less through authoritarian demands. Finding a balance in you and your children's disagreements, stay firm on your views, but allow for your children to question you when they see fit because it allows for more clarity. The more comprehension kids retain about drug use and the effects related to it the better the odds for avoidance of it.

Meditation and connectedness to God can be a valuable source to assist parents combating drug usage. Meditation is a skilled breathing and concentration exercise that enhances mental clarity and allows for individuals to make more calculated decisions. Sarah Bowen, an assistant professor and author, created a relapse prevention program taught through meditation with the purpose of implementing a useful method for former addicts to utilize when temptation arises.

DO YOU FEEL NUMB YET?

"Mindfulness-Based Relapse Prevention (MBRP), which combines practices like sitting meditation with standard relapse prevention skills, such as identifying events that trigger relapse. Rather than fighting or avoiding the difficult states of mind that arise when withdrawing from a substance, this combination tries to help participants to name and tolerate craving and negative emotion" (Nauman, 2014).

Meditation involves an inner peace and resilience when it comes to negative influences.

"MBRP helps people to relate differently to their thoughts, and use tools to disengage from automatic, addictive behaviors" (Nauman, 2014). The whole concept of finding alternatives to cope with stress and negative influence is major to limiting or eliminating destructive behaviors.

Meditation is a highly recommended method to use to cope with issues or anyone seeking to get off drugs.

Perception, Drugs and Harsh Realities

Substance abuse being a major destructive behavior is not discriminatory. There is a stereotype that blacks are the only ones affected by drug abuse. This is due ineptly to crime, low income, depression, and systemic efforts to suppress black people. Majority of the conditions are present and true but there are other cultures at the mercy of drugs as well. Hispanic, Caucasian, Native Americans and Alaskan natives submit to addiction holding them in a chokehold for survival likewise.

"While about 60 percent of those admitted to publicly funded substance abuse treatment programs in 2008 were for white or Caucasian individuals, according to the National Institute on Drug Abuse (NIDA), the Substance Abuse and Mental Health Services Administration (SAMHSA) reports that minority groups or people of color may suffer from substance abuse or mental health disorders at high rates part due to difficulties accessing care, the right kind of care not being available, and environmental, social, and financial concerns may be barriers to treatment" (Sunrise House Treatment Center, 2019).

DO YOU FEEL NUMB YET?

Media manipulation such as that described earlier in this book has led many in the public to believe that blacks are the only group impacted by drugs. The above mentioned research falsifies these manipulations. Blacks have had to endure extreme repercussions for the conscious indulgence of drugs, creating a flawed perception by society, erroneous arrests, a lack of support compared to those of other races, and less resources and information all while battling alongside a corrupt legal system.

To further support the claim above, some astute studies have provided information:

"Studies indicate that the estimated rate of transition from drug use to drug dependence is not generally greater for African Americans, even for those living within inner city neighborhoods" (U.S. Department of Health and Human Services, 2003). This is tied to the theory that inner cities have the constant reminders of the long term and harsh effects of drug abuse due to their surroundings which aids in this statistic.

Additionally,

"African American high school seniors consistently have lower rates of licit and illicit substance use

compared with whites. This finding also is true among African American youth in lower grades, where less dropping out has occurred. Despite these findings, illicit drugs are a major problem in the African American community (National Institute on Drug Abuse, 1995). One reason for this is African Americans who use alcohol and other drugs experience higher rates of drug-related health problems than do users from other ethnic groups (Alcohol.org, 2020). Another reason is drug abuse is among a variety of long-standing factors believed to cause criminal behavior in African American communities" (National Institute on Drug Abuse, 1995).

And lastly,

"Studies on the prevalence of drug use among Hispanics indicate it is alarmingly high among adolescents and, because a large proportion of the Hispanic population is young, a larger proportion of Hispanics may be at increased risk for drug use (Johnston et al. 1991)" (National Institute on Drug Abuse, 1995).

This study also reported that Asians had the lowest percentage when it came to drug usage in the US. Hispanics

DO YOU FEEL NUMB YET?

were next, followed by whites, blacks and last Native Americans as well as Alaskan natives. To summarize, Native Americans led the way and whites had only a 1.5 % difference from black people in terms of drug usage. Overall, what we see is a major problem that is widespread.

"Asians/Pacific Islanders have the lowest prevalence of past-month use for nearly all drug categories across all age and sex groupings. The prevalence of any illicit drug use among racial/ethnic groups was 3.7 percent for Asians/Pacific Islanders, compared with 6.1 percent for whites, 5.3 percent for Hispanics, 7.6 percent for African Americans, and 11.3 percent for American Indians/Alaskan Natives. American Indians/Alaskan Natives had the highest prevalence of past-month use for all drug categories" (National Institute on Drug Abuse, 1995).

Disparities with regard to substance abuse among the many ethnicities truly complicates the grand issue. Since it has a vast impact, collectiveness is imperative. Along with the congruity of all cultures, problem solving to counteract against this problem is needed; instead, everyone is fighting their own issues within their demographic, mainly by race.

Education, Depressing Times and Faulty Interventions

A study by Meilman and colleagues interviewed about 6,100 students in HBCU's as well as white institutions, discovering that drug usage on the HBCU campuses were fairly low compared to that of white institutions (Meilman, Presley, & Cashin, 1995).

Typically overshadowed by grim media reports depicting black culture as drug dependent, researchers created an analysis from comparing black colleges to white colleges only to discover drug usage soared more in white colleges than black.

One of the biggest blowbacks to black communities has been the psychological fusion or association between crime, the black race, and drug abuse.

Not to devalue the effects of slavery and laws enacted to mislead, isolate and bind blacks, but the mere fact that there was a whole epidemic on crack cocaine which led to the dismantling of black families speaks volumes. Slavery, corrupt laws and total isolation of a human race made things severely worse. The fusion of crime and drug abuse among blacks was a passive but effective way to bypass these archaic, manipulative, and heinous issues perfectly colluding outsiders.

In return, it created archetypes of barbarianism, idiocrasy, and maniac beings in relation to blacks. The reality

DO YOU FEEL NUMB YET?

of it is that black people have been dealing with untreated anxiety, trauma, subjugation on multiple levels, having minimal economic resources, tirelessly worked community activists, and few laws aiding in the restoration of the culture. Worst of all, we have a historical recollection cultivated by radicals who rearranged the extensive history of their people.

Many blacks are not educated on the true history of their race. Instead, they are fed misleading information that damages their psyche, causing them to think that ignorance and intellectual, economic, academic, and social vulnerability are norms in black society. The issue of drug abuse aided all of the madness created and masked problems, making them less relevant to the rest of society. As to say tolerated:

"Historical adversity, which includes slavery, sharecropping and race-based exclusion from health, educational, social and economic resources, translates into socioeconomic disparities experienced by African Americans today. Socioeconomic status, in turn, is linked to mental health: People who are impoverished, homeless, incarcerated or have substance abuse problems are at higher risk for poor mental health" (Mental Health America, 2020).

In addition to this,

HASE TREK

"Despite progress made over the years, racism continues to have an impact on the mental health of Black/African Americans. Negative stereotypes and attitudes of rejection have decreased, but continue to occur with measurable, adverse consequences. Historical and contemporary instances of negative treatment have led to a mistrust of authorities, many of whom are not seen as having the best interests of Black/African Americans in mind" (Mental Health America, 2020).

More importantly, adequate help is desperately needed to help resolve these issues.

In retrospect, as opiates began to infect and dominate suburban/rural communities, the response has been as American-like as ever. Active approaches to aid non-minority communities were in full effect from the time that the devastation began penetrating until today.

From a spectator's view, an emotion such as anger can deeply burn into one's soul to witness such a disproportionate care or lack of humility with regard to such a matter of life. Meanwhile, it voicelessly communicates that your life as a black person is not an essential to humanity or mankind. As a voice within the community, witnessing such heroic tactics and pro-activeness with the opium and fentanyl dominance in non-

DO YOU FEEL NUMB YET?

black neighborhoods became disheartening in a sense for black communities, who received a completely opposing response with the "Crack Era".

Truly embodying all of which I choose to disregard to harness my frustrations on a very intimate topic. Families are still working to undo the carnage dispensed by a white, rigid, and highly addictive pebble. Severely depressed lives, all products of the crack cocaine era and the chaos that resulted because of it. Circa 80's being the worst decade of all.

Eventually, a solution was provided to assist the youth in prevention for future purposes, so drug use would decline: **D.A.R.E**. and newer legislature reprimanding black communities associated or populated with drug abuse.

Disregarding the facts that when you're living in overcrowded spaces, with inadequate nutrition, recreational violence, lack of funds and resources, denying participation in recreational drug use may become very difficult for many. The first lady of the 80's, a white suburban woman, had an intention to simplify a big problem.

D.A.R.E., a "Drug Prevention" program based around giving insight of distinct illegal drugs supported by case scenarios displaying negative effects of these drugs by amateur actors as well as having spokespeople attempt to persuade the youth to be different when it came to peer influence also to combat gang violence which as we see today has only intensified the problem and became popularized in media.

Just beyond the 25 desks with chairs, centered around calendars, math charts, assorted vocab words and student projects engulfing the 360-degree circumference of the room, there lived a world opposite the vibe of the school. A hopeless despair in which an individual tried to find an association between their school life and the outside world, but they never seemed to mesh. Henceforth, that educated classroom was once a safe haven though the home life was a shifted reality. Seeing the popularity behind drugs within communities was befuddling, for the sake of a kid attempting to create their path. Interestingly, William Colson, a psychologist, in '98 argued that D.A.R.E. increased drug awareness, but not in the way that was intended:

"The reasons for D.A.R.E.'s failure are summed up by the words of the psychologist William Colson, who in '98 argued that D.A.R.E. increased drug awareness so that "as they get a little older, [students] become very curious about these drugs they've learned about from police officers" (Wolchover, 2012).

In agreeance, an awareness is a doubled edged sword, especially in this case. Awareness of this manner can mislead and misinform. For some teens, it led to propelling them to

DO YOU FEEL NUMB YET?

want to try the very drugs they were told to stay away from. The awareness raised by the program wasn't solely positive in its influence. Unfortunately, the curiosity about drugs for teens was in many cases reinforced.

Quite Numb

Presently, opium and fentanyl are the new drug "CRISIS". Causing an elevated casualty rate, ravaging white suburban communities like a relentless whirlwind. Claiming countless lives and causing anguish within white families.

A strong coil gripping tighter and tighter in suburban communities. That grip is all too familiar. This crisis is kin to a rather mature beast, upholding extensive occupancy for quite some time in black communities across the nation. Both cultures can relate to the exhaustion, fueled by the initiative to regress the damage that arises because of this mystical beast's destruction.

Drug addiction, the beast, willfully claiming souls as collateral and sparking mass awareness of its ever-increasing presence. From the 60's, the beast was introduced to black communities and by the 80's, the beast had been acquainted heavily.

DO YOU FEEL NUMB YET?

Present day, this current beast is heavy-handed like Mike Tyson '86 with a vengeance to outdo its predecessor. The pantheon of political leaders viewed the chaos and decided that a logical tactic would be contain the people fending off the beast and not the beast itself. Unsparingly, drug addiction continues to infiltrate communities without any resistance, resulting in an inescapable plague on both sides of the war.

Once that beast strikes and latches to its prey, every man for himself is full force and devastation ensues. Drug addiction cripples neighborhoods once it infiltrates and its visual reflection in the community is as surreal as it gets.

This representation and reality has opened the eyes to a world which many refuse to accept. Leading many to have a blind eye when dealing with urban community circumstances. Simply ignoring. As a response to the oblivious denial, which led to crack pillaged "ghettos", the second coming was inevitable because there lacked real repair - just a patch job to cover up the havoc corroding cities. Creating the perspective of what we would call "hoods" nowadays.

Simply put, un-treating and un-attending to urban, black or lesser class issues made it inevitable that an issue within the higher economic classes would come at some point. Fentanyl, opioid and heroin crises are at the foot of the major drug epidemic. Another extension to the list of drug issues that reside in many cultures. One of the worst ever was the shift from heroin in the 60's to crack addiction in the 80's. That 20-

year period of intense, hardcore drug use did its damage. These two eras equate to numerous decades of adversity plus the aftermath that resulted from it.

With the introduction of this new beast, the heroin epidemic alongside the opium craze, comes the resemblance of the old beast, crack addiction. The style is unique, but the motives are identical, and the target is newly appointed for this drug-driven beast.

The focus is on white communities' economic, health and social elements while counteracting this epidemic. We see that hardcore drug use such as heroin impacts the jobs one works or the performance one gives. The outward and inward quality in terms of health and the social representation it has on the white culture, the damage done because of the family or loved one's investments in supporting the habit, curbing the habit, or strategizing against it because of the addiction their family faces is difficult as well as devastating. Drug addiction is a cataclysmic force.

In 2016, the Opioid crisis stepped in and made its mark. Instead of implementing a plan on the people, the legal system began raising instant awareness and deploying resourceful tactics to curb the terror opioids had created in white suburbia. A very logical and precise plan to a rather perplexing problem.

The action plans the government put in place was genius to help battle the opioid crisis. Implementing more rehab

DO YOU FEEL NUMB YET?

centers, making it about mental health, utilizing the THC/CBD craze to be an ally in the quest to stop the synthetic and hard drug usage.

    Black communities have adapted and overcome a lot of the damage from the crack era, but the work is not complete. A lot of years of trauma occurred as a result of the 80's. Was the expense of the conditions black communities faced during the drug crisis of the 80's beneficial to those of the current crisis? Or is it that the leaders in power realized a major mistake was made during the Reagan administration? These are some the questions that comes to one's mind.

    The 80's drug crisis was a trap on both ends regardless of whether you were a user or dealer. Many who either were users or dealers of the beast currently struggle to re-acclimate themselves in communities because of either the legal lashing for their participation in the movement or the strength it takes to deny a strong addiction. The positive initiative to stop dealing and/or using becomes challenging for those who have dealt with a legal charge or spent time in jail for their intimacy with crack. Always bound by their past and not accepted for their present nature. There's no surprise when one resorts to old tactics to cope with oppression.

    The majority of our adjacent white communities will not have to fret or raise an eyebrow to such repercussions for their mishaps. As for our fellow black neighborhoods, we can say that the struggle with drugs has led to many complexities.

The bondage of drug addiction will be fought on the behalf of white people, granting them the proper rehabilitation and re-entry into society. Resources will be exhausted and sought to deliver the outcome the white community seeks.

The Origin and History of Drugs

Growing up, drugs seemed to just be there, never realizing that everything has an origin. I think tracing back to the origin and history of drugs is important. To be involved in a movement and to produce successful results, comprehending the past can reshape the future if done so with intent and focus. Below, I will provide an overview of the history of some of the most impactful drugs in society today in relation to the numerous drug crises along with general knowledge of a few other drugs.

Theorists suggest that opium was discovered as early as 3,400 B.C within the Southwest Asian region. Opium was originally considered to be a recreational drug. Referred as the "joy" plant to the Sumerians (inhabitants who resided in southern Iraq region).

"The earliest reference to opium growth and use is in 3,400 B.C. when the opium poppy was cultivated in lower Mesopotamia (Southwest Asia). The Sumerians referred

DO YOU FEEL NUMB YET?

to it as Hul Gil, the "joy plant" (Drug Enforcement Administration Museum & Visitors Center, 2019).

Unlike the other joy plant (weed) that many people love today, Sumerians discovered opium and capitalized off of the plant, ultimately networking with Assyrians (inhabitants who lived in the northern Iraq region) and wound up aligning with Egyptians. From then the Egyptians (inhabitants of Africa), then created and sustained such a hierarchy with in society by granting the ability to maximize the benefits for health purposes and personal reasons. The drug became widespread through the vast ranges of land. Opium had quickly gained the world's attention (Drug Enforcement Administration Museum & Visitors Center, 2019).

Opium was largely found along the Silk Road, justifying the Opium war in the 1800's in China. The Silk Road is a series of interconnected routes that ran from Europe to China in the 18th-century. A series of trade routes developed between the empires of Persia and Syria on the Mediterranean coast and the Indian kingdoms of the eastern hemisphere. By the late Middle Ages, the routes extended from Italy in the West to China in the East and to Scandinavia in the North (Drug Enforcement Administration Museum & Visitors Center, 2019).

Tea created in China had a major demand within the British parliament, to acquire the funds to make the purchase.

HASE TREK

Britain illegally smuggled opium into China through the East India company and used India (the vessel) to flood China with opium. The effect became rising addiction rates and displacement for individuals leading to immigration into the United States, bringing such an influence into the land through railroad development and major extraction of gold in California, stamping the Gold Rush (Drug Enforcement Administration Museum & Visitors Center, 2019).

Opium as stated is a plant, residing in mountainous territory. It demands dry, warm climates for full development. Asia is a modern day inhibition for opium ranging from Turkey to Pakistan is where it is harvested and cropped. Opium dens, distinct locations, were established as hubs to buy and sell opium. Dens reportedly were found in China, Southeast Asia, the United States, and parts of Europe.

More recently, opium has been grown in Latin America, notably Colombia and Mexico. Masterminded by the likes of drug lords Pablo Escobar and Joaquin "El Chapo" Guzman have been considered powerhouse players in the distribution and wealth within the Central and Southern Americas. Farmers throughout both Asiatic and South American regions provide the distribution and sale of the product legally and illegally (Drug Enforcement Administration Museum & Visitors Center, 2019).

In more current times, opioid addiction has intensified. In the US there has been a spike in overdoses and a spike in

DO YOU FEEL NUMB YET?

death due to the opioid crisis. Studies shown that more than **"70,200 Americans died from drug overdoses in 2017" (Rettner, 2018).** Yet in 2019, just two years from such a steep death rate which unfortunately likely has increased, **OxyContin accounts for almost 94% of all opioid use in the U.S.** Opioids are distinct from heroin, an opioid derived from the poppy plants having a stronger opium base.

OxyContin is orally preferred. Versatile enough to be crushed and snorted or dissolved in water and injected, to allow flexibility for the user. As a college student, many of my peers who were of a different ethnicity engaged in the snorting activity of OxyContin pills because of the instant impact and rush it delivers to the body.

Often I'd wonder why these people felt tempted to engage in use of such an intense, deadly drug. Coming from my community it was seldom to see any of the youth snorting or injecting any drug. I knew we all had been traumatized by the crack era whether one admits it or not. Drug prevention became essential.

Indeed, one believes it was the cigarette butts scattered throughout the block, crushed glass bottles on the pavement, the 45-degree angle where the bodega rests, home of the drug traffic, loud mouth, rambunctious, flamboyant crews idling at the entrance/exit of store fronts as their consumer straggles along in dire condition to get that hit that, this sighting turned many youth in my city away from hard drugs.

HASE TREK

All too common on plenty of corners in the urban cities. On a daily, this was what city residents were confined to by default. Whether they spoke out of their mouths or their body expressions reflected it, they sought to one day be able to get away from it. Especially because it became so generational to witness this... almost like the twilight zone.

Whether you live in the hood or have traveled through the hood, this is an obvious sign of the type of community you are in.

Much has changed from the 80-90's in terms of the existence of the crack addict. In today's time, the addiction has transitioned. The inner-city struggle now is that of the prescription drugs and cough syrup addiction. The Opioid Crisis. So frightened by the virulence of crack-cocaine but blinded mentally from seeing that the popularized designer drugs aka prescription medicine are engineered medicine derived from the same drugs their elders participated in.

Cough syrup and Percocet's are the new wave of preferable drugs. Cough syrup or Promethazine Hydrochloride/Codeine Phosphate or known on the street as "Hi tech" has seen a surge in sales with the influence of the hip hop culture. Artists have been promoting and hyping up the usage of cough syrup.

The syrup is usually mixed with a sweet, sugary drink to allow for smooth consumption. As early on as Pimp C to Lil Wayne, hip hop artists are commonly associated with the

DO YOU FEEL NUMB YET?

highly potent drink. Among the likes, rapper Future has been another huge advocate of the drink and the Percocet's as well seemingly making references such as "Perkys be calling me/Going Codeine crazy". Enticing as it sounds to drink… think again, the side effects of this drug are menacing:

"Increased sleepiness/Bowel problems including constipation or stomach pain/ Increased intracranial pressure/ Feeling dizzy or light-headed/ stiff muscles /confusion sweating changes in pulse, heart rate, and blood pressure" (Cunha, 2018).

In addition, Percocet's severe conditions include:

"Blood clot in vein /depression/giant hives/hallucination/hepatitis caused by drugs/hives/inflammation of skin caused by an allergy/life threatening allergic reaction/lung failure causing loss of breath/problems with circulation/rash/shock/short periods of not breathing/stevens-johnson syndrome" (Cunha, 2018).

The side effects of both drugs are quite scary but beyond that is the potential for fatality which is a sure reason to avoid these drugs. Death as we've viewed, has grasped plenty of people, more distinguishably our celebrated musicians such as Pimp C, DJ Screw, Lil Peep, ASAP Yams and Mac Miller.

At what cost are we willing to pay for your struggle? Don't let it be your LIFE.

Deaths involving psychostimulants - Adderall, Ritalin and the like, rose independently from those in combination with synthetic opioids. As inundated as opium is documented to be, experts who discovered opium essentially implemented it within our culture for health purposes.

Opium has been used in pain relievers, sleep inducers and bowel movers, along with other uses. Currently, the primary opium circulating in the US is manufactured and regulated in pill form. Morphine, extracted from opium resin, has a high potency and also reveres as a go-to for intense pain. With the capability of offering major temporary relief to the user. Morphine administered professionally is usually orally or injected into an IV. Codeine, kin of morphine and derived from opium alike, is another manufactured, distributed and regulated substance usually in liquid form prescribed for pain relief in conjunction with cough suppressing. Codeine has a lesser fatal calculation in comparison to its opium affiliate.

Contrary to the negative stance on opium, seeds extracted from the poppy plant provide an appetizing experience on items such as poppy seeded bagels, lemon poppy seeded cakes. These edible items have extremely low to no effect on individuals. Consumption of poppy seeds could

DO YOU FEEL NUMB YET?

put one at risk for contaminated urine if required to submit a urinalysis, however.

    I strongly encourage one to practice caution when indulging in poppy seeds. Despite its few positive usages, opium use still impacts numerous lives negatively and should not be endorsed.

    Coca, which matures into cocaine, rooted in South America, is an intensely addictive drug that is processed in jungle laboratories where the coca is extracted from the leaves, birthing cocaine. Due to its chemical make-up, cocaine is a highly addictive drug that the body processes as a stimulant. Because the body begins to rely on the stimulant, there are long-term health problems that individuals may suffer from. These problems include stomach ulcers, severe depression, inflammation or palpitations of the heart, and bleeding in the lungs. Cocaine can also affect the functions of the brain and its ability to regulate stress and mood.

    Until the early 1900s, cocaine was commonly used in Western medicine as an anesthetic because of its numbing ability. However, in the 1960's cocaine became widely popular as an expensive, exotic drug of choice for consumers as well as addicts. Disco junkies, the free-spirited individuals, synthesized cocaine with their party movement.

    Cocaine had aggressively expanded throughout the US well into the 80's. Cocaine's expansion allowed for dealers to experiment with different ways to increase euphoria, to increase profits and welcoming more availability and cheaper redistribution. Eventually leading to the creation of crack cocaine from cocaine which involved mixing, boiling water, adding other chemicals with a sufficient amount of cocaine, and including baking soda to bind all ingredients together creating a rigid rock shape. Dealers broke pieces off the crack rock, packed the substance into nickel bags or small glass vials, and generated revenue.

    Freeway Ricky Ross would be heralded the originator of cultivating the crack rock movement (Johnson, 2011). Though it's still debatable. He was estimated to have grossed up to $3 million at the apex of his movement as he stated on his Vlad TV interview (VLADTV.com, 2015).

    Ross' fate would be that of many other black men within society: prison enrollment. He was sentenced to 27 years, completing 20 years before his release. Black communities, like other communities, had recreational drug use but majority of blacks in the late 70's and early 80's were working-class individuals and business owners.

    The introduction of crack allowed for mass distortion among black people, mass incarceration of black men, lack of resources to support addicts efficiently, police brutality due to lack of comprehension of the epidemic, government dependent families resulting from the many single parent homes, alarming death rates, a rise in crime in multiple areas and other disheartening struggles that would ensue.

DO YOU FEEL NUMB YET?

There are those of us that may read this and ask the question of how a drug can have this type of influence and cause these types of issues. Shouldn't the people be able to make better choices? In order to understand the answer to this question, one has to understand that many black people have never truly had power over their own circumstances. Blacks not having sound foundations to aid, protect and ensure that their communities were afforded opportunities and equity hurt us greatly. Being able to come from dark times of slavery then prosper for decades was major, yet later only to succumb to the forces of drug addiction and criminal justice legalities shifted the culture.

Even with the grace period when blacks were doing well economically they still had to face the tactics of real estate agents who set them up in areas that were detrimental to their economic and social ascension. As mentioned below,

Many blacks began seeking better opportunities confined to specific residential areas and conditions, "After World War I and continuing into the 1960s, a massive wave of African Americans migrated to cities in pursuit of industrial jobs. They were forced into a few increasingly crowded, dilapidated neighborhoods through violence, restrictive covenants (from 1900 until a 1948 Supreme Court decision), and discriminatory

practices by real estate agents. Meanwhile, white families were moving to segregated suburban areas, especially following World War II (Wilson, 1987)"

Once displacement and confinement are established as well as accepted we get to see firsthand how the conditions of those being displaced subjugated and limited them from further ascension out of poverty ultimately.

Poverty births negativity and mainly reinforces negativity because if one doesn't not have the resources to explore environments outside of poverty it becomes the only reality known.

For those from the inner city, think about relatives who are shuffled through the criminal justice system, those who only go from "hood to hood". These types of circumstances are easily accepted. When everyone else around you that looks like you goes through similar, if not the exact same issues.

"Poverty and long-term joblessness have been associated with a constellation of other negative consequences, [including] overcrowded housing, poor physical and mental health, despair, post-traumatic stress disorder, family dissolution, teen pregnancy, school dropout, interpersonal violence, crime, and drug and

DO YOU FEEL NUMB YET?

alcohol abuse, among others. These factors help perpetuate disadvantage across generations. Some of these factors are the direct consequences of structural disadvantage. Others involve personal volition, particularly those regarding sexuality, relationships, violence, and illicit drug use. Hence, there appears to be a clear cultural (or subcultural) basis to these behaviors" (Dunlap, Golub, & Johnson, 2006).

With this separation of living and social conditions, blacks now are able to see how the rest of society can separate itself from their culture. Many do not want to acknowledge the truth of the matter which has been an ongoing battle for black communities with aspirations to receive the proper resources socially, economically and politically.

Default Family

"The use of extended kin networks among low-income African American households was prevalent in the late 1980s. They found many single mothers had very active extended kin (and fictive kin) networks. They also found that many of the households were characterized by continual changes in family composition due to new relationships, births, and deaths" (Dunlap, Golub, & Johnson, 2006).

When it specifies extended kin, we talk about siblings that have different dads and moms or the aspect of how when as a child, your mom was friends with someone so long that they claimed to be your aunt and their kids became your cousins. Not by blood. Traditional family makeup was not a custom anymore - family became more than just blood relatives due to dismantling of the black family.

"Since 1960, the percentage of African American children living in two-parent households plummeted from two-thirds to a low of one-third in the mid-1990s (U.S. Bureau of the Census, 2004). Conversely, the prevalence of African American children living with their mother only increased from 20% in 1960 to over 50% in the 1980s and 1990s. The prevalence of white children in mother-only households also increased from its historically steady level of 6% (Ruggles, 1994), but by 2002 still comprised less than 20% (U.S. Bureau of the Census, 2004)" (Dunlap, Golub, & Johnson, 2006).

The above-mentioned statistics are self-explanatory as we actually are, know and have heard of the many black

DO YOU FEEL NUMB YET?

households governed by single mothers and absent dads. Fifty percent is a very high number of single mother households. Lack of male leadership was a serious problem which ultimately confused generations upon generations in terms of the role of a man and how a man is to conduct himself independently.

ALL STEMMING FROM A DRUG. LET THAT SIT A SEC...

While problem after problem forms, eventually there has to be a solution in the works. Yes, this solution started from the inside of black communities.

Special individuals became committed to helping families combat drug abuse and the issues stemming from drug abuse. We were able to see examples through groups such as the Black Panther Party, NAACP, NOI and other groups in the black community against drug abuse, social disparity and criminal justice practices detrimental to black communities.

"Actions express priorities." Mahatma Gandhi

Even with the support of different groups in black communities, the drug presence still was forceful and evident. One must acknowledge the courage, fearlessness, and leadership involved in tackling a huge conundrum like drug abuse. Between the rapid spreading of drug addiction and

HASE TREK

laws countering its possession and use, communities were in a binding space.

Laws of Numbness

In today's society most of us know or have heard about the metrics of drug laws in place currently. If we don't know the narcotics law, we've seen the action of the narcotics law because of personal experience, close relatives or strangers who have been involved with it through their use or distribution of narcotic drugs. The identification and information associated with various diverse drugs contributes to the intricate criminal laws passed to enforce penalties.

The first known drug law enacted in the US was a city ordinance passed in San Francisco in 1875 to try to stop the spread of opium dens (Drug Enforcement Administration Museum & Visitors Center, 2020); this was a time where opium was a popular drug because of its various uses.

Opium addiction has tremendously grown as an addiction within all communities. Popularity lately increased in the black community. Even with the decline of crack cocaine and heroin. Newark, alongside many large metro areas, has large involvement in opium and prescription pill abuse. Serious stuff, and the death rates tied to these drugs are just as serious.

"By 2017, the greatest level of synthetic opioid involvement in opioid-involved overdose deaths was among blacks in all metro areas and ranged from 67.4% in medium/small metro areas to 74.8% in large fringe metro areas" (Lippold, Jones, Olsen, & Giroir, 2019).

In connection, heroin indulgence, due to the high magnitude of euphoria experienced, has increased more in suburban, white communities, anchored by the addition of Fentanyl laced heroin. Fentanyl is a synthetic opioid and is 50 to 100 times more potent, as referenced by the Centers for Disease Control and Prevention (2019).

By 2010, heroin had begun increasing its death toll:

"From 2010 to 2017, rates generally increased for each of the racial/ethnic groups shown, with the highest rates observed for non-Hispanic whites. In 2017, the rates were 6.1 for non-Hispanic whites, 4.9 for non-Hispanic blacks, and 2.9 for Hispanics" (Centers for Disease Control and Prevention, 2019).

DO YOU FEEL NUMB YET?

Cannabis, or weed, a plant, possibly has grown in popularity among many demographics. Heavily associated with black communities, weed or marijuana, interestingly enough is shown to be mostly consumed by young adult white men,

"Of all the demographics ranked, the population most likely to use weed are young white men" (Hugo, 2018).

Alongside, is the stat that young people in general use weed the most,

"18- to 25-year-olds, use weed the most (29.6 percent). So though we see that young white adults consume weed the most; Young adults in general prefer to smoke weed; about 30% of the nation" (Hugo, 2018).

Adults determining to engage in drugs is significant but even more significant is the kids or young adults limiting their full potential through early drug use. Plenty of reports as stated in this book discuss the hindrance early drug consumption can have on the developing minds of adolescence and teens.
Parents and teachers stay aware!

When I think of such things as kids indulging in narcotics or drugs, I strongly agree that laws to regulate drugs are needed. The contrast for me is the types of penalties in place for those who violate the laws.

As humans, we understand that we differ in many ways and that people change. People do make mistakes and the severity of the mistake should be considered, but the conundrum for me is the moral aspect in allowing drug dealing or usage to bind someone to 100s of years of jail time. When it comes to drug dealing we must understand that it takes two to complete a transaction. Beyond the resources we have in store for those addicted, resources to alter drug distribution would be great too. Law revisions would help if things like this were considered in different ways than they are currently.

Statistics, information and data play a large part in legislation made in resistance of the over population, consumption and spreading of drugs in the US. For those who may not have much understanding about various regulated drugs, below are the different schedule drugs and rankings according to the DEA (United States Drug Enforcement Administration, 2020). The following drug schedules are listed on the DEA's site.

Schedule I drugs are considered to have no medical use and have a high potential for abuse. Heroin, Crack cocaine, LSD, and marijuana meet the criteria.

DO YOU FEEL NUMB YET?

Schedule II drugs are those which have been documented to have high probabilities for addiction but that have some accepted medical uses. They include cocaine, methamphetamine, opium, and highly controlled prescription medications like morphine and oxycodone.

Schedule III drugs are quoted to have a lower potential for abuse and may not be physically addictive, involving greater radius for uses. Drugs in this category include anabolic steroids, ketamine, Vicodin, and certain products containing codeine.

Schedule IV are mostly prescription medications that maintain low potential to be abused. On the contrary, if abused, addiction is both physical and psychological. They include Xanax, Klonopin, Valium, and Ativan.

Schedule V: These are medications that have a low potential for abuse over the counter drugs like Robitussin.

As previously explained, all drugs listed have been categorized by the DEA, which is a law enforcement agency who regulates, enforces the criteria for the uses of the drugs and attack parties who illegally use or distribute the types of scheduled drugs.

Three-strike laws and mandatory minimum laws have both contributed to the sharp increase in the number of people in prison for drug offenses. Enacted by the Clinton administration, the three-strike rule applies to an individual being convicted of felonious crimes on multiple occasions.

HASE TREK

The third time conviction delivers a lengthy prison sentence to the convicted criminal.

As a tie-in to drug consumption and abuse, individuals convicted on narcotic offenses became felons. Those felons who were not able to find better solutions after being convicted struggle to re-acclimate themselves properly within society, leading to more issues like a third strike. A system such as this is quite logical for someone like a serial murderer, rapist or some other sort of malice-driven individual, but it makes much less sense in the case of drugs.

I acknowledge we are always free willed and we are to be held responsible for our choices, yet addressing problems without well-planned solutions really contributes to the problem. With a consistent, widespread problem adversely affecting an ethnicity with a distinct color, effective implementation was and is a must.

Contemplate… having to do extensive jail time due to personal consumption or even selling of drugs. Meanwhile… when you do get out, the necessary resources to help you find a more productive means to reestablish yourself are bleak. One of the reasons why we see individuals getting recycled in the system.

Do I condone drug dealing? Hell No! However, I do see how when options are limited and education is limited, hopelessness and desperation can make someone act in ways that are irrational.

DO YOU FEEL NUMB YET?

In addition to individuals being arrested for drugs alone, possession of drug paraphernalia can lead to jail time too. Paraphernalia includes any equipment, accessory products, or materials meant for the use, creation, or concealment of illegal drugs.

Convictions for such vary and don't hold much volume in terms of jail time as compared to the user's drug preference. Primarily the conviction consists of a misdemeanor charge. This is if one is a user. Drug dealer's paraphrenic equipment contrarily, in conjunction with federal drug laws, sustain a hefty conviction charge if convicted of being in possession. Paraphernalia possession may not be as serious of a crime as the actual possession of a drug, but federal law considers it to warrant arrests penalties. Scales, bags for packaging purposes, grinders, crack pipes, etc, are all prime examples of paraphernalia.

When it comes to distribution or manufacturing of drugs, ignorance isn't enough to allow individuals to be dismissed from the matters, even if they honestly are unaware of being in the presence or vicinity of them. If a raid, traffic offense, or a simple disturbance call is placed, any party present during the time that the drugs are discovered or recovered is considered to be a part of the allegations, regardless of cognizance.

Seldom used as an effective defense for this type of participation, there is a legal defense called **unwitting possession** which allows for a person to prove they were not aware or conscientious of the drugs which were discovered, i.e. in a car, home or other location according to FreeAdvice (2020). Conviction rates for possession of illegal substances are quite high, which makes proving unwitting possession exceedingly challenging in a court of law.

On a larger scale, the **4th amendment**, protecting citizens from illegal search and seizures does allow for individuals who may have been found in possession of an illegal substance to not face jail time because the officer on duty illegally, without consent, searched a compartment or distinct location that is used for storage.

Trunks, glove compartments and even in some cases homes without a warrant or consent, officers are restricted if told by the citizen to withdraw from searching. If an officer does not adhere to the individual's request, they are to be dismissed from matters pertaining to the allegations or charges.

Proving one's innocence is very challenging, especially because of the different variations of possession of drugs. Physically having any illegal substance warrants for an actual possession charge. Meaning on your person, in pockets, bags, or even in your hand. Having cognizance or knowledge of any illegal substance within close proximity while not physically possessing the substance is considered constructive possession. Actual and constructive possession

DO YOU FEEL NUMB YET?

are prosecutable offenses that allow for individuals to be convicted in either circumstance.

Possession, an abstract term, becomes extremely decisive based on the volume of the highly controlled substances. For instance, if found in possession of marijuana, the fines and allotted jail time would differ than if found with Percocet pills. This is on the basis of addictiveness, severity if abused and extreme rarity to access these types of drugs because of limited manufacturing of the drug along with distribution. Which stem from the rankings in the schedule of drugs.

In addition, federal law enacted by the Reagan administration allowed individuals in possession of 1 gram of crack cocaine to be considered to be equivalent to possessing 100 grams of pure cocaine leading to a mandatory five years on the first offense with a maximum of 40 years.

This is wrong as well as perplexing after analyzing the mathematical disproportion in sentencing of illegal substances. Factor in an offender of a specific ethnicity and the wrongness shell-shocks even more. That these harsh penalties impacted melanated communities was unquestionable. The structure of the culture would take a significant hit. Drug interest and activity levels elevated from the 60's well into the 80's. Drug laws in place at the time began to successfully over-reprimand blacks in the penal system, recirculating and concealing them for extensive periods of time. Costing so many individuals their freedom and rattling many households, causing numerous difficulties in family dynamics.

Dealing or possessing illegal drugs is not worth it! Think about it. Who wants to be inside a prison for a drug which only brings you anguish? Or worse yet, welcomes and coincides with the high fatality rate in the city? Death and jail are not the things to aim for. Be more mindful and please - weigh your options!

Returning to the discussion of drug addiction, some ways to rid oneself of drug addiction are simply by going cold turkey or through the deliberate process of rehabilitation. Both involve going through withdrawals, cravings and extreme body discomfort. Drug addiction is not a simple-fix ailment; rehabilitation is a process that helps to reform the habits of individuals. Many go to rehab, but rehab, as discussed, is a tedious process which involves a strong will and consistency. Most of those who go to rehab are estimated to relapse within the first year. **According to US News writer Castaneda (2017), 40-60% of people who get treatment for substance abuse relapse**.

Relapsing is almost a sure shot for first time rehabilitators. Yet it is POSSIBLE to overcome. Rehabilitation,

DO YOU FEEL NUMB YET?

if successfully completed, has great benefits. Better health, physical appearance, opportunity to generate more money and limitless growth in life if the drive alongside the energy is put forth.

Give it a try when ready and be ready to fight for what you really want!

A cocoon maturing into its beautification from a blanketed shell of internal struggle, eventually metamorphosizes into the vibrant, energetic, physically captivating butterfly. Though drug abuse is attached to stigmas of lesser, filth, chaos and lower standard of life, there is much beauty that comes from the ugly makeup. The plight of such a struggle shouldn't be used to portray fictitious truths to realistic stories. These are the ones who are daily living with an ultimately good choice turned bad.

There is truth in a substance abusers' journey, likewise for the reformed substance abuser as well. Knowing so, we must be non-judgmental and understanding even if people don't agree with the users' actions. Usually when someone reforms from abuse, there becomes a clarity in one's perspective. Allowing for more conscious decision making, once the addiction is diminished. Both sides were revealed to me through my own life experience. I was able to distinguish the two personalities of a drug addict and a non-drug addict by noticing mannerisms as well as tendencies.

Those relatives that were strong willed enough to go through rehab were able to display new or re-shaped bad habits transforming into more positives in their lives.

By acquiring her license to drive, earning her associate's degree in the midst of working toward completing her bachelor's, still actively involved with her grandkids all while maintaining employment for over 12 years, my aunt Vee has been a true pioneer. Resurrecting her life and progressing to reach her full potential, she chose to by facing her addiction and committing to her will-power.

Witnessing such perseverance also allowed me to see the contrast among other individuals within my family who haven't been able to channel such a forceful energy within.

Since the tender age of two, my father has been absent from my life due to drug addiction. During my journey, I'd often wonder how such an unimportant, invaluable poison could have such a grasp on one's being. Causing internal chaos for me, my half-sister, my mom and even my dad himself.

Allowing for him to elusively tread through the same city as me but still be unseen. Unseen to me and even the common people of the world because we know that drug addiction transforms people into transparent beings which no one wants to acknowledge.

DO YOU FEEL NUMB YET?

Thus, a major reason why you see people disrespect them in a manner that is quite disheartening. Loss of identity, humanity, seemingly absent from the race of life. Thirty years a pawn in the game that has done nothing but cause pain, anguish, sadness, and depression only to compromise one's mental health, the elements of life my dad as well as many are facing on a daily.

Prevention Education

With the epidemic of drug addiction residing in urban communities for an extensive period of time, collaborative prevention is required. Education pertaining to illegal drugs in a thorough, logical manner would definitely assist in the prevention. Allowing for kids and parents to be educated effectively, keeping congruity between school and community.

Project ALERT specializes in applying the internet to a purposeful mission to connect drug education, abuse and prevention to the adolescent population.

"Project ALERT uses interactive teaching methods, such as question-and-answer techniques and small-group activities, which appear to be a crucial element in the effectiveness of this type of curriculum" (Ellickson, McCaffrey, Ghosh-Dastidar, & Longshore, 2003).

Additionally,

"Based on the social influence model of prevention, the Project ALERT curriculum synthesizes 3 theories of behavioral change: (1) the health belief model, which focuses on cognitive factors that motivate healthy behavior; (2) the social learning model, which emphasizes social norms and significant others as key determinants of behavior; and (3) the self-efficacy theory of behavior change, which views the belief that one can accomplish a task as essential to effective action" (Ellickson, McCaffrey, Ghosh-Dastidar, & Longshore, 2003).

To ensure that families are aware and addressing the social issue, this program allows parents to incorporate their experience and knowledge.

"The parental involvement activities include adolescent interviews with parents about their experiences with and responses to peer pressure, parent/child drug IQ tests that assess knowledge about drugs and social influences to use them, and oral reports on drug use consequences presented to the student's family" (Ellickson, McCaffrey, Ghosh-Dastidar, & Longshore, 2003).

DO YOU FEEL NUMB YET?

With regard to illegal drug law revamping inner cities impacted greatly by drug abuse, project ALERT would shift a lot of the damage done from past decades of wrongdoing. Such a program could benefit more communities that deal with drug abuse plus its stressors that are associated with it.

Religion is major in this country as well as throughout the world. One of the major commitments of religious organizations is to give back to the community. Religious organizations, in my opinion, applying more grassroots work to restore and aid in drug addiction rehabilitation is needed. Many years ago, we witnessed the religion of Islam, in particular the Nation of Islam, restore many black communities by speaking and offering services to counter the plague of drug addiction in the 60's-80's by infiltrating education and lifestyle change in jails and also actively participating in the positive development of black communities. God, the concept overall is essentially a key to inspiring or maintaining discipline to one's own life. Twelve-step programs for drug abusers and alcoholics even utilize the concept of higher power or God as a motivator to keeping participants invested as well as focused on their recovery.

Spiritual preservation too has helped individuals resist or prevent them from utilizing drug addiction to solve internal struggles.

Yoga, meditation, and creative arts are a few other tactics used to prevent or alter the comfortability of drug dependence. A great friend of mine in Atlanta, Georgia offers Yoga and meditation sessions to the youth as a way to introduce sound ways to deal with the daily stressors or life to combat the temptation to use drugs to avoid problems.

Another common approach for individuals reforming their lives are Alcoholics Anonymous or Narcotics Anonymous meetings, which have aided those in need of being held accountable for reclaiming their lives and the community of individuals do an awesome job of accepting one's true nature regardless of the circumstances by its unchanging and open arms policy.

Rarely do we get a glimpse of such a crucial developmental program that does such. Having the opportunity to sit in on a meeting, the acceptance of the user owning up to their addiction while putting forth ACTION to curb their addiction is courageous. The reasons, the will and the perseverance within recovering substance abusers guides them to reaching their full potential which is key to their solitude.

Beyond all the extensive information and theories behind drug use, distribution and possible solutions, the most valuable key to all of this is tapping into the mind. Aligning parallel minds that create innovative ways for individuals to handle life stressors and internal or external pressures.

DO YOU FEEL NUMB YET?

To change the addict/abuser is to reform the dealer as well.

Ideally, since both parties operate off the basis of each other, once the abuser's mind state is reformed, then the dealer has no other option but to change as well. Which from my bias, begins to void the importance of illegal substance consumption.

In this plight to accurately understand and relate to the drug abuser, I had to go to someone with a history of involvement. This inspired the idea to conduct a few interviews which would help to eliminate any outsider biases.

Understanding that we all have unique stories, the conclusion was drawn to conduct a few interviews of individuals who had or still have their battle with drug addiction. The next chapter contains the participant responses and my reflections of intimate and authentic interviews conducted with a few amazing individuals who graced me with their visceral perspectives.

Who Else Is Numb?

Each of the interviewees mentioned in the next section were conducted in informal settings; however in order to protect the identities of the participants, I chose to use aliases for each individual.

Mandy is a relative of mine who has been in the clutches of drug addiction since before my birth. I've known no other version of her, and I've become accepting of her. Beyond her personal struggle with drug addiction, she has educated me a lot on drugs, and that is without a conversation on the matter. Her actions have given me much of the information I possess about drug addiction. For the first time in my life, I figured it was time for me to hear her speak in regard to her truth. Delightfully, she openly gives her raw insight on her drug addiction.

Juug is another valuable interview. As I was dropping my son off to my aunt's home in the downtown district of Newark, I figured this was a highly populated area with people

DO YOU FEEL NUMB YET?

struggling with addiction. Instantly, I noticed that there were three men located under the tree shade, "grooving" off of their preferred substances. I approached the men and asked, "Who would want to participate in an interview about drug addiction?"

The first man objected and stated he only struggled with alcohol addiction. Eliminating himself. The next gentleman reluctantly objected and declined to speak on his addiction. So with all my eggs in one basket, I maintained hope that the last gentleman would participate. This man was quite buzzed. Right eye visible, left resting under the left eyelid. Head slowly descending to a specific level thus reaching that limit that it caused his head to sharply ascend back up awakening him like an electric jolt.

Again, I asked, "Would you be willing to talk about your drug addiction?" He snapped out his high briefly and said, "Yeah, I'll do it."

El Jay was the final interview. El Jay, a brilliant mind. Initially, I was supposed to drop my cousin off at home, but he wanted to detour. He directed me to a park in the citrus city region, Orange, New Jersey. Noticing group clusters of black men vibing, smoking, drinking, relaxing in the park, I was introduced to many of them by my cousin. Keeping it brief until I met El Jay.

Quite vigilant with his tall stature, Malcolm X frames and the respect that I saw he garnered among his peers. Upon greeting him myself, my cousin stated, "Remember you said you wanted to interview people about drugs? Talk to El Jay. He's the man." I was ebullient internally. El Jay readily agreed to converse about it. So, we took it from there.

Numb Society

- **When do you recall your first time using hard core drugs?**

Mandy - (Pupils directed to the ceiling, partially in a squint. Chin resting in the palm of her right hand, Pacing back and forth in the kitchen)…
"I would say I was in my 20's. Your grandfather introduced dope to me. My thing prior to this was drinking Bacardi and beers. I smoked some weed time and time but as far as the good shit, dope. My 20's definitely."

(My eyebrows raised in utter surprise)

Juug - (On the curb, resting his rear region and in a dopenated trance slowly nodding resembling a crane's dual movement)… "Trapped by dope; I'd say it was about 21 years old. Shortly after a time where I got shot in the groin area and the bullet got lodged in the upper thigh area into the muscle.

DO YOU FEEL NUMB YET?

First I was prescribed pills, morphine for the pain but yet they ain't do much to suppress the pain. They made me feel real mellowed. One day I ran into one of my partners from street running and I was headed home with my cane. He told me to hop in and he would drive me to the house. I hopped in and he was telling me how he had something for the pain.

I said, "What."

He pulled it out, had it on a matchbox in a dollar bill. Said, "Take a bump of this."

"Fuck no I'm not doing that shit," I said.

Then he told me trust him, and that it would ease the pain.

I was hesitant at first then said "Fuck it." I took a sniff, then asked him what it was.

He said, "Dope."

Soon as he said that I threw up all over the car. Then I hopped out the car.

Next thing I know he was yelling, "Oh shit! Juug look, You ain't using ya cane."

I said "Get the fuck outta here. My cane right here."

"Naw Juug - look inside the car."

Once I found out it stopped the pain, I used it every time I felt pain or thought I did. Shit even when I wasn't, it became continuous."

HASE TREK

El Jay - (Stationed in the center of the parking lot, tall statured, mound of dreads flowed down his shoulders, Malcolm X frames) "Man... I started shooting dope because of peer pressure back when I was 17 years old. I was down in Virginia State, a dorm room with these two chicks plus another dude. We was supposed to drink and chill then as we were chatting it up, my boy took out the dope and the needles, and no questions was asked - we just participated. Coming up in that era it was common to shoot, so though I wasn't into it, it was easy for me to want to try. From that point on I started shooting up."

The first experience for each of these individuals seems as though there was always an introduction by another person who was familiar with the drug of addiction. This person was always well trusted and familiar in terms of association. There was not much conversation involved before all individuals' tried drugs for the first time. Lack of questioning and further research seems to be a red flag before most individuals' first time usage. Juug did try to resist a small bit but things still led to a different result.

Noting that all participants were with their friends or relatives when they were introduced them to drugs. Sadly, most introductions did not come with much reluctance. Peer pressure, as referenced earlier, overruled any aspect of their

DO YOU FEEL NUMB YET?

moral compass when it came to the first-time drug usage. None of the participants had initially tried drugs after age 25, which is stated to be the age where the brain is able to organize, rationalize, and to be fully developed allowing for less impulsive decisions to be made.

- **What does/did it do for you?**

    Mandy - (rapidly chewing gum, arms folded in a horizontal stature) "The best sleep. I never slept that good in my life. The high was peaceful if you get me. Nothing compared, not even a weed or drunk high" (Mandy had such a joy when even speaking on her initial experience).

    Juug - (drifting in and out between both worlds, swaying in an absent rocking chair, sobering for a quick moment) "After I was shot, dope eliminated the pain that I had to deal with. Dope did what those prescription medicines couldn't do. The pain left and though the dope was doing more damage than anything; it felt right." (Juug has a powerful voice that overrules his appearance when he talks, beyond giving his experience, I see myself almost in his shoes. Honesty exudes from that same voice engaging me more with each answer to each question).

HASE TREK

EL Jay - "After shooting the dope in that college dorm, the after effect was best. I fell asleep good as fuck. Mind you we had the chicks there with us and I was supposed to do my thing with the one chick and wound up dozing off" (a subtle chuckle). "It had me from there on for quite some time" (Narrating to me, as he prolongingly tranced at the ground, almost as if he was placing himself at that moment once again. The low monotone voice he spoke gave me a vibe that he always seemed so mellowed out).

Pain relief and sleep were common factors that made their experiences pleasant. It makes one wonder how they slept prior to their drug abuse. Was there some discomfort before, or was it simply the easiness to sleep?

One thing I noticed is that no one quite thinks of the later struggles to come in that moment of serenity from the basis of drugging. Getting high is the thing of the moment until… as we see, many of those moments will calculate to some expense which they will eventually be responsible for.

Quality sleep or good rest can be achieved through other means than drugs. Sleep is a crucial component to health: "The National Sleep Foundation recommends getting seven to nine hours of sleep a night, the average American logs only six hours and forty minutes" (Asp, 2013).

Melatonin supplements are considered to be an alternative to illegal substance abuse: Melatonin, a hormone

DO YOU FEEL NUMB YET?

that controls sleep according to Asp (2013), is a supplement that is in neighborhood drug stores or health stores.

For more natural sleep, people can try caffeine reduction, working out, creating a habit of falling to sleep at consistent times each night, and changing one's diet.

As exercise enthusiast, I can agree that working out tires the human body and relaxes it in an effective way. Research supports this idea:

"Exercise reduced time to fall asleep by 55%, total night wakefulness by 30% and anxiety by 15% while increasing total sleep time by 18%" (Mawer, 2018).

Consider more natural and health effective ways to treating your sleep issues. Drugs are not the answer.

What losses have you taken as a result of drug usage?

Mandy - (deep sigh) "The loss of being around the kids. Then the judging, disrespecting and they don't even know. You lose a lot; people don't understand what's happening. People just think that you are being selfish." (There is a pain and regret in her voice, when speaking on her mishaps from choosing drugs over her responsibilities. That pain turns into desire to convince me that the other family members' perspectives toward her are wrong. Voiding or suppressing their truths, prioritizing her viewpoint).

Juug - (Extended pause, noise sounding of a car ignition cranking in efforts to clear his throat, softly he spoke) "Naw, no losses man." (I become somewhat confused based off of his circumstances as to whether he understood my question, so I reiterate the question. (Retracting his initial answer followed by)… "A lot of losses; shit I had a good job. I lost my family too. Too many man, and the shit is just crazy" (Followed by another sober pause).

El Jay - "No major losses other than myself. I was not fully dependent on dope and I was still very young, so I didn't lose nothing too serious" (Said with ease and casually. Confident that his addiction had caused no major losses).

Family adversity caused by their mistakes was felt in their words and declined vibrancy in their demeanor. Mandy being a relative, I firsthand saw the challenges faced by my cousins while she fought her battle at a distance. As far as Juug, his addiction did wear down his family ultimately straining relationships and losing relationships as well. El Jay's addiction did not tarnish his family in any way.

DO YOU FEEL NUMB YET?

- **How about the financial aspect, the money loss behind doing drugs?**

Mandy - "Oh my God - couldn't even imagine. In my lifetime over 30 years; could you imagine? Initially I started with a $20 bag of dope" (Pacing back and forth in the kitchen). "Shit if I think about it, I burned up a house or two; a lot of money. Other people's money, working money, you name it."

Juug - (beads of sweat racing down his face, met by an open palm swipe) "Aww man, man the money - I ran through so much of it. I have a $75 habit a day minimum. I once had a job, years ago and lost that too because this shit was weighing me down. But yeah a lot of money."

El Jay - "I spent a few dollars on it man. But I always had a somewhat of a hold on it so my habit ain't cost me nothing crazy. (Suddenly a comrade of his dropped a platter of food, causing him to say, "Damn you clumsy", then deep bass laughter. Then snapping back to the question), "Lots of people spend crazy amounts of money on dope. That fix they need requires it."

The money wasn't an issue to them. They were very knowledgeable and cognizant of the massive amounts of income they spent on their usage. The intriguing part is that they willfully found ways to get the money daily to support that habit. It's why you will see people with addiction issues do plenty of odd jobs because it's the quickest way to support their habit.

- **What are the effects of your drug of choice?**

Mandy - "Any ailments, it masks it. Damage of the body, not eating, exercising makes things become more intense" (The level of awareness of her health was interesting. Mandy, blind in one eye, has dealt with the health issues involved with drug addiction. At times in a moody state when she had not received her fix, a rage and anger that is absolutely different from her personality when she is high. An imbalance she could barely control within herself).

Juug - "I think it changes everything. The plus was the pain from the gun shot - it takes it away temporarily. The feeling of being high eases things. But if I'm-a talk bout the bad stuff, the moodiness when you don't have ya fix. The lack of care for the stuff everybody do like hygiene. Eating too, this shit control a lot."

El Jay - "Well it slows you down. Messes up your priorities. It damages the body a lot too. Skin color, posture

DO YOU FEEL NUMB YET?

and all the features of the body. I was blessed to not have done it for a long time."

The harmful effects on the body were something they all agreed on. Mandy said something intriguing in reference to dope masking her sicknesses if she had any.

As I begin thinking about the neighborhood addicts, I realize it is common to see neighborhood drug abusers tally up a long life. Contrarily the dealers tend to have shorter life spans. Crazy right, but it's the reality of the drug war in urban communities.

Drugs are vicious. The fact that we are able to see the physical destruction of it and be conscious of that fact internally damages you just as effectively. The participants in this interview are not pictured, but the condition two of the participants are in are not good. Yet, they are only two of many who are consistently at the whim of drug abuse.

Discolored skin, missing teeth, darkened circles around their eyes, very raspy voices, yellowish red eyes and dingy outdated garments. Lesser than hope, the notion that comes to mind, pity and sadness resonates more. One can only imagine the internal health especially because doctor visits are not the norm.

Think about this: drugs are not worth your health or physical appearance.

HASE TREK

Think of how good it feels to look good and to be in good health. Is this worth a risky experience?

- **What regret do you have?**

Mandy - (without a hesitation) "Regrets, is kids, the way they are and assume shit. They never been through the worst, though it was crazy for them. It's a part of the life we choose" (The assumption that her problem is merely just her problem seems to be a theme. Not ever thinking of the trauma that was inflicted on her own kids who had to live quite uncommonly because of her lack of involvement in their lives. It makes me think - does Mandy pity herself, or accept the fact that her kids have done well for themselves so they should have no issues with her? It's all interesting to think about).

Juug - (a calculated response, sobering awakening for the moment) "Ever picking it up in the first place. The losses that I had to go through, family, job and the struggle it puts you in" (Much of Juug's struggle seems to be from the lack of trusting his first instinct. It's as though he dreamed more beyond his current state and that though he accepts it, the feeling of being unaccomplished resides with him).

El Jay - "Yes I do regret ever using it" (a pause for a sec). "You know, at that time it seemed like the thing to do,

DO YOU FEEL NUMB YET?

especially growing up in the 60's and 70's. Like I told you before, I started doing it around age 17 and having to graduate from high school was hard. I did get my diploma, went to college for a little. Then wound up going to the war. Hiding the fact from my family that I used, then going to the war, where they let us use because it was so crazy over there. You had to be discrete with it but they knew we were getting high. To finally being able to get myself off it. Which was the best thing to happen to me" (A relief displayed in the brief widening of his cheekbone structure completing a smirk).

    A somber and humble demeanor was displayed in all participants when reflecting on the liability of the addiction in their lives.
    Self-love is important, and when you compromise it for a meaningless impulse, you show how much you care about yourself.
    Drug addiction and family doesn't co-exist well. When people abuse drugs, they tend to avoid quality care for their kids due to the thrill of getting their high. Even when one doesn't have kids, they still have to deal with their family's image of them and the liability they cause for the family due to the negative circumstances drug addiction binds them to. Who wants to have people talk down on them or to have things locked away every time you come around?
    A uneasy feeling? You bet it is.

Another reason to stay away from drugs.

- **Were any rehab programs attended and do you recommend them?**

Mandy - "Yes I attended," (arms intersecting, forming an X, hands tucked in between her armpits she quickly descended them to parallel alignment resting on the side exterior of her garments), "it wasn't helpful. I went to please people rather than for my own will. If I'm determined to not use it, I know what I have to do. You can give it up anywhere. A lot of people give up better in jail because it's a mind thing. When I did go, I never experienced any major symptoms. It's tough. As soon as you get out of rehab and hit the streets, the urge increases. But to anyone who wants to do rehab, it has to be when they want to for sure."

Juug - "I went to rehab about 4 or 5 times. Honestly, it didn't help me at all. I struggled every time I got out" (Silence, as he faded into that distance phase before...) "I always seem to wind up relapsing and back where I started. I would say try it if you want to find a way to get help with this shit. But for me it didn't do nothing to help" (drifting back off, under the shade of tree leaves).

DO YOU FEEL NUMB YET?

El Jay - "Me, I didn't do rehab. I prayed to God. For me I knew it was time and I prayed every day to God and I just stopped. I thank God for helping me too. See I was a surface drug user, so I wasn't full in deep with dope. I didn't make it an everyday thing. As far as rehab I cannot vouch for it because I never went."

Rehab's effective recovery tactics lacked relevancy in producing positive outcomes for the participants within this dialogue. That's not to discourage or shame the positive results that many do receive from the intense, committed hard work applied in rehab centers and programs.

Though rehab may not have been as effective for these individuals, likewise it is effective for many others. Alternatives such as meditation, recovery coaching, therapy, intensive outpatient programs, supplement and nutrient therapies, and harm reduction are all recommended methods to reduce or stop drug abuse according to Lux (2018).

- **Do you foresee a future with or without it?**

Mandy - "Pretty much for me this is it" (Confidence diffusing from her). "I enjoy getting high - just wish I could have been able to have balance and do the things I needed to for my family and myself" (Yet a sadness submerged the atmosphere, almost as she knows she was not able to establish nor manifest such an ideal desire).

Juug - "I don't know; right now I know that I'm stuck in my ways. I would love to one day be able to give this up and live the life of my dreams, but the truth is I am here, so I don't even know" (Such a question decreased his high. Suddenly his eyelids separated causing his second eye to open, now staring at the ground in contemplation).

El Jay - "I'm just thankful I never let it take a hold on me. I ain't going back and I been clean for over 20 years so I'm keeping God in my corner and continuing to live my life as best as possible and healthy as possible."

- **What advice do you have for the next person attempting to overcome drugs or who even fathoms starting to use?**

Mandy - "Whatever you do, try to think in a positive manner. You got to make a plan. You not gone get off it until you ready. You got to do it when you feel it in your heart. Be considerate of who you do it with and think wisely how you do it and how people will treat you."

DO YOU FEEL NUMB YET?

Juug - "Simply, DON'T DO IT! Drugs ain't no good and they cause too much pain."

El Jay - "If you really want to stop, stop, but do it with God. Samson was able to kill all those people after he asked God."

El Jay's response stuck out to me because he repeatedly mentioned throughout his interview how his belief in God anchored his will to want to change for better. El Jay's desire to overcome his circumstances with added with belief in God became his achievement.

The Wear Off

To those in the community, numb to the fact that substance abusers are within their communities because they see no value for them or do not share the same likeness of their lifestyle, there is much that can be learned from another person's trials and tribulations. These people in the community are simply people like the rest of us who go through what we go through and have more commonalities than we can measure beyond our naked eye.

As flawed as we are in this life, there is always this thing called change that guarantees us an alternative to all our mishaps. We can accept change, or we can set it aside until we see fit. The thing about change is that it is always prevalent and important. There is a study about the number 7 in relation to change, and to paraphrase, "Every 7 years an individual's likenesses will have changed due to their maturity." This is from a different perspective, yet it is relative

DO YOU FEEL NUMB YET?

in the aspect of change, which is to come regardless if we consciously move toward it or not.

To the many people who feel subdued by their addiction, you are the change. Hopefully one day you find that courage to change for the better and find a purpose to break out of your shell.

I understand things are not easy to do in life and that with any strong commitment comes a strong resistance to that commitment as well. The resistance doesn't define you; the resistance is merely your test to your commitment. One can do some amazing things when they see their purpose beyond their obstacles. Just find the inspiration within. Every big accomplishment started out a just a thought and if that thought is there for you to change then it is time to react to that change.

Never think it's too late. Plenty of people have reached their full potential at later stages in their life; with their victories, they demonstrate that one can overcome the hurdles of life challenges. Since one endures these life challenges already, it's best we use them for the better. There is plenty that one can do with their adversity. I once read a quote that stated:

"Adversity is your money maker."

HASE TREK

A quote I feel we all can relate to. We deal with so many issues in our lives. Most of the time, we spend more time reflecting on our issues than counteracting against them in the best way possible.

One thing to keep in mind is that beyond all the statistical and analytic data that was applied in this book, the reality of the situation is that it means nothing unless the notion to better oneself is a driving force.

The devastation that families have endured with the infiltration of drugs is disheartening and takes a lot of togetherness among the family to rid itself of the effects resulting from drug addiction. The positives of overcoming something as troubling as drug addiction can be prevention for future generations, a drive for individuals to aid others who go through a similar struggle, and a fresh start to create better generational habits, plus many more.

Drug addiction hit my family on both sides intensely. Some family members, I have only known to be that of an addict. As a kid, it was all too normal. As you mature, you see the distinctions between your family and other healthy families. Though the addicts in my family were barely around, they cared much for my cousins as well as my well-being. They had their internal struggles, but they tried their personal best to maintain their genuine personalities.

As a kid up until manhood, I often questioned and wondered why they didn't at least try or commit to getting

DO YOU FEEL NUMB YET?

right. As the days as well as time progressed, I became more intrigued by the fact that they had been committed to something so detrimental to their livelihood and their legacies within their family. My relatives missed a lot of crucial moments for their kids, grandkids and other relatives that they can never relive again.

Stevie Francis Davis, whom I love dearly, is truly an inspiration behind me wanting to understand this thing more and more every day. A charismatic guy to all the people that he meets. The thing that bothered me for years about him was that with all the people rooting for him and fighting for him, he did not have a fight for his own self. Ideally it had to be on his time and rightfully so, I have to respect that though he created me, we all are only responsible for our lives. I would love the day to see him along with many other relatives fix their situations, but the sad fact is that they may leave the soil of Earth not ever reaching their full potential.

Though you may think it's too late, that's not true. Think of the impact you can have without letting something control your very being. Especially if you have kids, you must fight at least to be the best you can be for yourself as well as for them.

Acknowledgements

This book came to life due to the many components involved.

First I'd like to thank the interviewees for allowing for me to gain insight on their lives by offering such intimate information. The Esprit de corps on all levels was fulfilling and super amazing because it allowed for this challenging subject to attain and retain fluidity. The courage that it takes to allow for oneself to be vulnerable enough to discuss their own grievances with the world is paramount. Drug usage is no joke. As we have seen or experienced within our own families or communities, I'm sure we as humans can all agree that we need some more solutions to this issue. Families are still heavily impacted with the burden of having to deal with such complexities correlated to drug abuse. Some families have yet to repair from the deep-rooted drug infestation that ravaged through their relatives.

HASE TREK

Like an untreated disease, until there is a cure initiated to counter react. That needs to be had. The family infrastructures will continue to suffer within the grasps of such a beast. Uneasily this sits in the mind, for the future generations of those affected are destined for an uphill battle. Though the timing may differ from the actual moment of change, we must continue to fight for that change. Don't disregard those in need of guidance and second chances. Be the gleam of light they seek to relieve them from the consistent tides of gloom.

"God doesn't need to punish us, we punish ourselves."

Lastly, to the ones who badly want to free themselves from the restrictions of drugs. Feeling mellifluously contrite, while working myself up to vociferously emphasize the words, **NEVER GIVE UP, FIGHT. FIGHT.FIGHT.** However the distance, you must go. Become victorious in your battle. **Persevere!**

Peace, Love and Prosperity- HASE Trek

References

ABC News. (2010, October 30). ABC News Network [Television Broadcast]. New York, NY: American Broadcasting Company.

Aamodt, S. (2011, October 10). Brain maturity extends well beyond teen years [National Public Radio]. Washington, D.C.: National Public Radio.

Adams, M. (2017). Five ways parents can prevent drug abuse. Retrieved from https://whitesandstreatment.com/2017/04/18/ways-parents-can-prevent-drug-abuse/.

Alcohol.org. (2020). Race demographic statistics on alcoholism & treatment. Retrieved from https://www.alcohol.org/alcoholism-and-race/.

Anderson, R.N., & Smith, B.L. (2003). Deaths: Leading causes for 2001. National Vital Statistics Reports, 52(9). Retrieved from https://www.cdc.gov/nchs/data/nvsr/nvsr52/nvsr52_09.pdf.

Asp, K. (2013). 8 Natural remedies that may help you sleep. Retrieved from https://www.health.com/condition/sleep/8-natural-remedies-that-may-help-you-sleep#95439.

Castaneda, R. (2017). Why do alcoholics and addicts relapse so often? Brain chemistry plays a major role. Retrieved from https://health.usnews.com/wellness/articles/2017-04-24/why-do-alcoholics-and-addicts-relapse-so-often.

Center on Addiction. (2011). Adolescent substance use: America's #1 public health problem. Retrieved from https://www.centeronaddiction.org/addiction-research/reports/adolescent-substance-use-america%E2%80%99s-1-public-health-problem.

Centers for Disease Control and Prevention (2019). Mortality data. Retrieved from https://www.cdc.gov/nchs/nvss/deaths.htm?CDC_AA_refVal=https%3A%2F%2Fwww.cdc.gov%2Fnchs%2Fdeaths.htm.

Centers for Disease Control and Prevention (2019). Synthetic opioid overdose data. Retrieved from https://www.cdc.gov/drugoverdose/data/fentanyl.html.

Cunha, J. P. (2018). Percocet. Retrieved from https://www.rxlist.com/percocet-side-effects-drug center.htm.

Didenko, E., & Pankratz, N. (2007). Substance use: Pathways to homelessness? Or a way of adapting to street life? Visions Journal, 4(1). Retrieved from https://www.heretohelp.bc.ca/visions/housing-and-homelessness-vol4/substance-use-pathways-homelessness.

djvlad. [VLADTV.com]. (2015 December 17). Freeway Ricky: I've had days where I've made $3 million. [Video file]. Retrieved from https://www.youtube.com/watch?v=MxgNBzip2BM.

Drug Enforcement Administration Museum & Visitors Center (2019). Cannabis, coca, & poppy: Nature's addictive plants. Retrieved from https://www.deamuseum.org/ccp/opium/history.html.

Drug Enforcement Administration Museum & Visitors Center (2020). Stop 6: Enforcing the new drug laws. Retrieved from https://www.deamuseum.org/idatour/enforcing-the-new-drug-laws-6.html.

Dunlap, E., Golub, A., & Johnson, B.D. (2006). The severely-distressed African American family in the crack era: Empowerment is not enough. Journal of Sociology & Social Welfare, 33(1). Retrieved from https://www.ncbi.nlm.nih.gov/pmc/articles/PMC2565489/.

Editors, History.com (2017). Just say no. Retrieved from https://www.history.com/topics/1980s/just-say-no.

DO YOU FEEL NUMB YET?

Ellickson, P.L., McCaffrey, D.F., Ghosh-Dastidar, B., & Longshore, D.L. (2003). New inroads in preventing adolescent drug use: Results from a large-scale trial of project ALERT in middle schools. American Journal of Public Health, 93(11). Retrieved from https://www.ncbi.nlm.nih.gov/pmc/articles/PMC1448059/.

Farrow, J.A., & Schwartz, R.H. (1992). Adolescent drug and alcohol usage: A comparison of urban and suburban pediatric practices. Journal of the National Medical Association, 84(5). Retrieved from https://www.researchgate.net/publication/21660834_Adolescent_drug_and_alcohol_usage_a_comparison_of_urban_and_suburban_pediatric_practices.

FreeAdvice. (2020). What does the term "unwitting possession" mean and is it a valid defense? Retrieved from https://criminal-law.freeadvice.com/criminal-law/drug_crimes/unwitting_possession.htm.

Glanton, D. (2017). Race, the crack epidemic and the effect on today's opioid crisis. Retrieved from https://www.chicagotribune.com/columns/dahleen-glanton/ct-opioid-epidemic-dahleen-glanton-met-20170815-column.html.

Greene, J.M., Ennett, S.T., & Ringwalt, C.L. (1997). Substance use among runaway and homeless youth in three national samples. American Journal of Public

Health, 87(2). Retrieved from https://www.ncbi.nlm.nih.gov/pmc/articles/PMC1380799/.

Hugo, K. (2018). Young white men are smoking the most legal weed, study says. Tech & Science. Retrieved from https://www.newsweek.com/people-these-jobs-are-most-likely-use-marijuana-least-colorado-885625.

Johnson, S. (2011). 'Freeway' Ricky Ross, the drug kingpin who ignited crack cocaine epidemic. Retrieved from https://www.mercurynews.com/2011/01/16/freeway-ricky-ross-the-drug-kingpin-who-ignited-crack-cocaine-epidemic/.

LaFrate, A. (2015, March 23). American Chemical Society [Video Broadcast]. Washington, D.C.: American Chemical Society.

Lippold, K.M., Jones, C.M., Olsen, E.O., & Giroir, B.P. (2019). Racial/Ethnic and age group differences in opioid and synthetic opioid-involved overdose deaths among adults aged >/= 18 years in metropolitan areas – United States, 2015 – 2017. Weekly I, 68(43). Retrieved from https://www.cdc.gov/mmwr/volumes/68/wr/mm6843a3.htm.

Lux, K. (2018). Sobriety Tips & Tools: 9 Alternatives to rehab you can start today. Workit Health. Retrieved from https://www.workithealth.com/blog/alternatives-to-rehab.

Mawer, R. (2018). 17 Proven tips to sleep better at night. A Holistic Guide to Health. Retrieved from https://www.healthline.com/nutrition/17-tips-to-sleep-better.

Meilman, P.W., Presley, C.A., & Cashin, J.R. (1995). The sober social life at the historically black colleges. The Journal of Blacks in Higher Education, 9. Retrieved from https://www.jstor.org/stable/2962645?seq=1.

Mental Health America (2020). Black & African American communities and mental health. Retrieved from https://www.mhanational.org/issues/black-african-american-communities-and-mental-health.

National Coalition for the Homeless (2009). Substance abuse and homelessness. Retrieved from https://www.nationalhomeless.org/factsheets/addiction.html.

National Institute on Drug Abuse. (1995). Drug use among racial/ethnic minorities. Rockville, MD: National Institutes of Health Division of Epidemiology and Prevention Research.

National Institute on Drug Abuse. (2019). Marijuana. Retrieved from https://www.drugabuse.gov/publications/drugfacts/marijuana.

National Institute on Drug Abuse. (2014). Principles of

adolescent substance use disorder treatment: A research-based guide. Retrieved from https://www.drugabuse.gov/publications/principles-adolescent-substance-use-disorder-treatment-research-based-guide/introduction.

Nauman, E. (2014). Can mindfulness help stop substance abuse? Greater Good Magazine: Science-Based Insights for a Meaningful Life. Retrieved from https://greatergood.berkeley.edu/article/item/can_mindfulness_help_stop_substance_abuse.

Rettner, R. (2018). US life expectancy dropped in 2017. Drug overdose deaths are a big reason why. Retrieved from https://www.livescience.com/64188-life-expectancy-decline-drug-overdose-deaths.html.

Stagman, S., Schwartz, S.W., & Powers, D. (2011). Adolescent substance use in the U.S.: Facts for Policymakers. National Center for Children in Poverty. Retrieved from http://www.nccp.org/publications/pub_1008.html#9.

Schwartz, Y. (2012). Painkiller use breeds new face of drug addiction. Retrieved from http://www.hcdrugfree.org/drug-alcohol-news/2015/2/13/painkiller-use-breeds-new-face-of-heroin-addiction.

Substance Abuse and Mental Health Services Administration

(2014). Table 19. Illicit drug use or abuse in the past year among persons aged 12 or older, by state and substate regions: Percentages, national averages based on 2008, 2009, and 2010 NSDUHs. Retrieved from http://www.samhsa.gov/data/report/table-19-illicit-drug-dependence-or-abuse-past-year-among-persons-aged-12-or-older-state-and.

Sunrise House Treatment Center (2019). Addiction among different races. Retrieved from https://sunrisehouse.com/addiction-demographics/different-races/.

United States Drug Enforcement Administration (2020). Drug scheduling. Retrieved from https://www.dea.gov/drug-scheduling.

U.S. Department of Health and Human Services (2003). Drug use among racial/ethnic minorities. Retrieved from https://archives.drugabuse.gov/sites/default/files/minorities03_1.pdf.

Williams, E. H. (1914). Negro cocaine "fiends" are a new southern menace; Murder and insanity increasing among lower class blacks because they have taken to "sniffing" since deprived of whisky by prohibition. Retrieved from https://www.nytimes.com/1914/02/08/archives/negro-cocaine-fiends-are-a-new-southern-menace-murder-and-insanity.html.

Wilson, W. J. (1987). The truly disadvantaged: The inner city, the underclass, and public policy. Chicago, IL: The University of Chicago Press.

Winters, K. C. & Arria, A. (2018). Adolescent brain development and drugs. National Center for Biotechnology Information, 18(2). Retrieved from https://www.ncbi.nlm.nih.gov/pmc/articles/PMC3399589/.

Wolchover, N. (2012). Was D.A.R.E. effective? Human Nature. Retrieved from https://www.livescience.com/33795-effective.html.

Made in the USA
Columbia, SC
16 October 2021